中華人文

CAL

CHINESE ARTS & LETTERS

杨昊成 主编

Editor in Chief: Yang Haocheng

译林出版社

No. 2 2018

图书在版编目（CIP）数据

中华人文. 2018. 第2辑：英文/杨昊成主编. —
南京：译林出版社，2018.10
ISBN 978-7-5447-7520-5

Ⅰ. ①中… Ⅱ. ①杨… Ⅲ. ①中华文化-英文 Ⅳ.
①K203

中国版本图书馆 CIP 数据核字（2018）第 210126 号

中华人文　杨昊成 / 主编

责任编辑　於　梅
装帧设计　韦　枫
责任印制　董　虎

出版发行　译林出版社
地　　址　南京市湖南路 1 号 A 楼
邮　　箱　yilin@yilin.com
网　　址　www.yilin.com
市场热线　025-86633278
排　　版　南京展望文化发展有限公司
印　　刷　江苏凤凰扬州鑫华印刷有限公司
开　　本　718 毫米 ×1000 毫米　1/16
印　　张　13.25
版　　次　2018 年 10 月第 1 版　2018 年 10 月第 1 次印刷
书　　号　ISBN 978-7-5447-7520-5
定　　价　88.00 元

Editorial Office of CHINESE ARTS & LETTERS

Editor in Chief : Yang Haocheng

Deputy Editors in Chief (alphabetically) : Jia Mengwei Josh Stenberg Liu Feng

Editors : Han Lifeng Xu Shiyan

Director of Editorial Office : Li Zhongtao

Edited by School of Foreign Languages & Cultures, Nanjing Normal University

Address: 1 Wenyuan Road, Huacheng Hall, Nanjing Normal University, Nanjing, P.R. China (210023)

Phone: 86-25-85891029

E-mail: chineseartsletters@njnu.edu.cn; chineseartsletters@163.com

Website: http://english.jschina.com.cn/chineseartsletters

Published by Yilin Press.

Address: Buiding A, 1 Hunan Road, Nanjing, P. R. China (210009)

Phone: 86-25-86633278

Cover Calligraphy: Yang Haocheng

Cover Design: Wei Feng

《中华人文》编辑部

主编：杨昊成

副主编（按拼音排序）：贾梦玮 刘 锋 石峻山

编辑：韩丽枫 许诗焱

编辑部主任：李钟涛

编辑单位：南京师范大学外国语学院

出版单位：译林出版社

封面题字：杨昊成

封面设计：韦 枫

地址：中国南京市湖南路1号A楼（210009）

电话：86-25-85891029

邮箱：chineseartsletters@njnu.edu.cn; chineseartsletters@163.com

网址：http://english.jschina.com.cn/chineseartsletters

Contents

Oct. 30
2018
VOL 6
NO. 2
TOTAL 10

Editor's Note

Editor in Chief
Yang Haocheng / 杨昊成

Starting this issue, *CAL* will branch out to cover our key writers across China and not just those active in Jiangsu Province. The first name that came to my mind was Jia Pingwa (贾平凹), a writer from Shaanxi Province, north western part of the country. I began reading Jia about thirty-five years ago when I was a new-baked teacher of English fresh from college. I was intrigued by the way Jia told his stories, all based on his intimacy with that land and its people. He seemed most adept at telling those stories with his distinct native dialect, and to someone like me from Jiangnan, south of the Yangtse River, his stories gave off an exotic flavor I never savored before. He was so fluent a raconteur and his tales were so full of color that when years later I happened to see him on TV, I was surprised to find that Jia Pingwa was in effect a very plain person, "a weak physical specimen of unremarkable physiognomy, a halting speaker," to quote one of his many critics, and did not seem to be very comfortable talking to people or answering questions put to him on the spot. I then realized that his world belonged at his desk where, shrouded in heavy cigarette smoke, and with all the window curtains closely drawn, he span one yarn after another about the land and the people he knew and loved so much. His pen has never stopped writing ever since he took it up for the first time, and over the forty-odd years of literary creation, he went through innumerable ups and downs and finally made a name for himself as an unshakably established writer. Strangely enough, unlike the sad trajectory of many writers' career that went from slogging uphill to reach the apex of fame to falling quickly downhill into the pit of oblivion, Jia Pingwa's career was more or less plain sailing. As he matured, he became more and more eloquent in his story-telling, and his literary and artistic interests even expanded to cover such genres and fields as essays, literary criticisms, calligraphy, and paintings, each harvesting for him unusual gains and fruits. One cannot but acknowledge that Jia is a born genius and he came to this world mandated by Heaven to present spiritual miracles to the people.

"Autumn" (秋天) is the third chapter of Jia Pingwa's fiction *Tiangou* (天狗), or the Heavenly Dog, a good-hearted, artless, diligent orphan. He was an apprentice to a master well-digger and was in secret love with his master's wife. Well past the age of marriage (he was thirty-six), Tiangou would brush off any match-making proposal by anyone, even by his eldest aunt, who swore that she would not die with her eyes closed if Tiangou did not get his better half. His heart was with his master's wife, an able, warm-hearted, and equally hard-working woman, the "Bodhisattva" in his eyes. One day, as fate would have it, the expert well-digger, an iron-willed craftsman and the backbone of the household, got trapped in a well-digging operation when a huge rock fell off and half-buried him. When Tiangou was sent for, he managed to negotiate the passage downward, and frantically pawing at the soil under the unconscious man, he finally pulled him out. Although his master was dragged back to life from the verge of death, the nerves below his waist were beyond repair and he became a useless lump. To help support the family, Tiangou consciously and constantly lent a helping hand, so much so that he gradually replaced his master to become the pillar of the family. The wasted man then had an idea; he wanted his wife to "marry anew to support the old," and the man he had in mind was none other than Tiangou, his son-like apprentice. Tiangou was in two minds about this; on the one hand, he felt his long-cherished dream would finally come true; on the other, he felt somewhat guilty if he should have his master's wife as his own woman. The trio, plus Wuxing, the couple's primary school kid, formed a new family in the end and began to live under the same roof albeit in an embarrassing way. It would take some time before they hit it off. The story is masterfully translated by Jun Liu (刘浚), one-time editor and journalist with *China Daily* and now a professional C-E translator residing in New Zealand.

"The Brick Bed" (土炕) tells of a barren woman who adopted a pregnant Eighth Route Army soldier who had strayed from her squad. The country woman waited on her like mother and sister until she gave birth to a baby girl Kitty. Then the female soldier left for the army, leaving her baby to the care of the country woman who took the girl as if she were her own flesh and blood. Kitty grew into adulthood, finally becoming a bureau chief in a big city. But when the Cultural Revolution came, she was sent to a reform school and, refusing to see her children suffer because of her, she decided to send her oldest daughter Xiuxiu to where she herself was raised by her foster mother. Two generations of mother and daughter were fed, nurtured, and raised up on the same large brick bed of the country woman, but both left for the city in the end, leaving the old woman all by herself to wither, shrivel, and die without making a stir in the world.

"Trees Can Talk!" is a simple enough story about an old stubborn man who, for fifteen years and three months, went petitioning to officials higher up that he owned a tree planted in 1948. All thought the man was insane, but he would not give up, claiming that "the tree can talk." His repeated failure to convince people of his "weird" idea led to the reinvestigation of his case by "I," a cadre in the local government, who was accidentally drawn into the picture. At long last, the wrong was righted, and he breathed his last, a good case in point of Confucius's maxim "In the morning, hear the Way; in the evening, die content."

Echoes of Classics of this issue does indeed feature Confucius and his *Analects*, perhaps the most iconic cultural embodiment of Chinese civilization. As a great educator, thinker, and founder of Confucianism, Confucius's stature and influence even surpass those of his mentor Laozi, and he has been ranked Number One of the "Top Ten World Cultural Celebrities." His dream, however, had been in the political arena, and that's why he and a few of his disciples spent fifteen years wandering from state to state as an "itinerant preacher," to quote Christoph Harbsmeier, trying to have his voice heard by the rulers and princes. Only when he met with repeated cold shoulders and even hostility did Confucius settle down in his homeland and devote the remaining years of his life to "teaching students regardless of their class distinctions." His talks mainly centered on politics, education, and human relations, and the key concepts of his preaching were loyalty, righteousness, ritual, wisdom, truthfulness, benevolence, the Way, Goodness, gentlemanship, and filial piety. Confucius is, however, a most humane, good-humored and humorous conversationalist, even a *plaisanteur*, quite different from the grim-faced moralist and ritualist later Confucianists helped to shape and uphold ever since Dong Zhongshu (董仲舒) of the Han and Zhu Xi (朱熹) of the Song dynasties. In other words, Confucius is much less Confucian for his multifarious characteristics, and above all, his humanistic sensibilities, as the text of the *Analects* well testifies.

Among the numerous

translations of this Confucian classic, we've chosen Burton Watson's version as a tribute to this prolific translator and Sinologue who passed away just last year. His rendition impresses me as faithful, fluent, informal, and colloquial, a far cry from either Arthur Waley's scholarly rendering, or James Legg's sometimes cumbersome interpretation which Gu Hongming (辜鸿铭) strongly disapproved of. Gu's own version, however, insightful and eloquent notwithstanding, is more often a paraphrase than a pithy translation. We've printed here the first nine excerpted "Books" of the *Analects* together with Watson's Introduction. Selections from the remaining eleven "Books" are to appear in the next issue.

"Clamour," an extremely sensitive piece of prose by Siren (塞壬), an equally sensitive author, tells us of the raucous and rowdy madding crowd that a restless soul has to grapple with in daily existence. Poignant and blazingly forthright, the essay lays bare before our eyes the true colors of various people struggling at the grassroots. So many grating noises, so many helpless scrambles, and so many sleepless nights. Standing amongst them, however, is an adamant, unyielding woman who is all ready to embrace even harsher realities.

Culture and Heritage of this issue features the Grand Canal, "an incredible marvel of the east." Consisting of four parts, the Introduction, the People, the Cities and the Cargoes, the four pieces are a detailed panoramic view of the Canal, of its history, culture, economy, geography, local customs and practices, and its inextricable ties with politics and rulership over the centuries. Printed here are the first two pieces and the other two will be published in the next issue.

Sheng Meibing (盛梅冰), a professor of oil painting from the School of Fine Arts of Nanjing Normal University, is a real gentleman. He is not the sort of Bohemian painters we commonly see around us, long-haired or bald, bearded or whiskered, drinking and smoking, and cynical about everything in the world; rather, he very often seems unperturbed, composed, and dispassionate. Yet there is an inborn dignity and a feel of aristocracy about his bearing. Meibing was born into a typical traditional Chinese intellectual family and has fostered a good taste ever since he was a child. This taste grows up with him, nurtured by environment, learning, and an intense interest in everything cultural, making him an unusual amalgam of the cream of both the East and the West. Meibing has a sharp eye for aesthetics; he is a genuine antiquarian, a practiced connoisseur, a censorious collector, a rare photographer, but above all, an oil painter whose palette mixes and concocts either a natural world he feels so ecstatic about, or his thinly veiled nostalgia for those lost "good old days."

Featured Author: Jia Pingwa

（贾平凹）

Jia Pingwa was born in 1952 in Dihua Village, Danfeng County, Shaanxi Province. He began publishing in 1974, and graduated from the Chinese Language and Literature Department at Northwest University in 1975. Jia is a current member of the National People's Congress, vice-chairman of China Writers' Association, chairman of Shaanxi Writers' Association, and editor-in-chief of *Yanhe* (延河) and *Meiwen* (美文) magazines. Published works include the 20-volume *Collected Works of Jia Pingwa*, and representative works include 16 novels such as *Ruined City* (废都), *Qin Opera* (秦腔), *Old Kiln* (古炉), *Happy Dreams* (高兴), *The Lantern Bearer* (带灯), *Lao Sheng* (老生), *Ji Hua* (极花) and *Shan Ben* (山本); short stories "A Woman Named Black (黑氏)," "Felicitous Site (美穴地)," "Wu Kui (五魁)"; and essays "The Ugly Rock (丑石)," "Three Chapters about Shangzhou (商州三录)," "Weather (天气)," and more. His works have won five national literature prizes, namely: Mao Dun Literature Prize, Lu Xun Literature Prize, the National Outstanding Short Story Award, the National Outstanding Novella Award, and the National Outstanding Essay Award. He has also received over 50 recognitions such as Shi Nai'an Literature Prize, the Chinese Media Literature Award, Bing Xin Prose Award, Zhu Ziqing Prose Award, Lao She Literary Award, and the Contemporary Literature Award, among others. Moreover, he has received the

Pegasus Prize for Literature in America, the Prix Femina in France, Hong Kong SAR's Dream of the Red Chamber Award — World's Distinguished Novel in Chinese, and is decorated in the French Order of Arts and Letters. His works have been translated and published in more than 30 languages including English, French, German, Russian, Japanese, Korean, and Vietnamese, and have been adapted for film, television, theater, and opera over 20 times. Jia Pingwa is one of the few great literary geniuses in China's current literary circles. He is one of the most rebellious and profoundly creative writers on China's contemporary literary stage, boasting wide-ranging influence and worldwide importance. He is also among the very few contemporary writers who could be enshrined in both Chinese and world literary history.

Jia Pingwa / 贾平凹

Autumn (an excerpt from *Tiangou*)

Jia Pingwa / 贾平凹
Translated by Jun Liu / 刘　浚

The third day of the ninth lunar month was Tiangou's birthday. He was born in the Year of the Rat, first of the Twelve Zodiac Animals. Tiangou was turning thirty-six and entering his inauspicious "Threshold Year," when taboos tail you like shadow and your heart is in your mouth with every action you take.

Come to think of it, Tiangou is rather pitiful. The Wang family is a small one, and with few relatives on the paternal or the maternal side, and distinguished ones scarce too, there aren't many left to carry on the lineage. Since his parents passed away, most have ceased contact. The rest who occasionally visit look down on Tiangou, and reckon he'll never amount to anything. Naturally, familial ties have grown thin as water.

Tiangou is the eldest nephew of his mother's brother, and his was the most heart-broken wail heard when his uncle passed. But when it came to authoring the funeral banner, Tiangou, the First-born Nephew, wasn't even in the running for the honor. The son of his deceased third aunt is a director in the county bank, and this gent has it all: a wife and a son, and the all-important *face*, so it was his name on that banner, not Tiangou's. At the time, Tiangou was infuriated:

When a man hasn't proven himself capable, does his seniority by birth somehow drop a notch? He knelt at his uncle's tomb and cried his heart out.

Ever since then, he has been emotionally close only to his eldest aunt, the last living sister of Tiangou's mother. Her time is overdue, but she's still hanging in there. "I'm just too worried for Tiangou's sake," as she puts it, and topping her worry list is her nephew's marriage. Seeing no hint of marital prospects while Tiangou was thirty-five, she's been panicking about his Threshold Year. "Be careful about each and every thing you do," she admonishes him at every chance, "don't let your guard down for one second." And she insisted that Tiangou celebrate the critical thirty-sixth birthday with fanfare, so the happy event would overpower the bad luck, and vanquish potential disasters.

In the end, the one who hosted the celebrations was none other than Tiangou's Shi'niang, his Master's wife. Three days ahead of the big day, she forbade her husband and his apprentice to do any well-digging. Come the third day of the ninth lunar month, she cooked up a lavish banquet, seven platters and eight bowls in all.

During the feast, his eldest aunt came from the other side of the river. She had been to Tiangou's place and found no one. Taken aback at the table laden with dishes, she was quick to pronounce a string of blessings, place her handmade noodles and fish-shaped dough on the cabinet, and present Tiangou with a loose-fitting blouse, a red belt and a crimson silk *dudou* belly-wrap. Being pampered like a baby upon its first birthday, the thirty-six-year-old cackled until he was breathless. As soon as his aunt left, Tiangou tried to regift these lucky charms to Wuxing, his Shifu's son. But Shi'niang pulled a long face and demanded that he don them then and there. She was dead serious, so Tiangou obeyed.

As Tiangou's year of peril draws to a close now, the old lady arrives again from across the river. Finding her nephew with four limbs intact, strong and sturdy, rosy and ruddy, she's as content as a devotee reciting the Buddhist sutras.

"Seems your destiny is a robust one. When nothing disastrous happens during your Threshold Year, the future is even brighter."

On that cheerful note, her prattle turns to the family lineage: Perhaps the Wang's won't come to an end after all. But then thoughts of her sisters, all of whom died ahead of their time, redden the rim of her eyes.

"Once your birthday is over, Tiangou, it'll be time to get things rolling with your marriage. The King of Hell has kept your auntie in this world, but unless she sees you tying the knot, she can't make her exit. Confide in your old auntie: Didn't you spot even one promising girl all last year?"

"Nope," admits Tiangou.

"Your auntie has got her eyes on one for you. She's a divorcée, but a very decent one. She has a three-year-old child, and she divorced just this spring. Might she please you?"

"Auntie, you must be going senile! I haven't even laid eyes on her. How do I know if I'd be willing?"

"Go on, spill the beans then. What sort of woman do you fancy?"

Tiangou hems and haws, but can't find the right words.

"What's there to be bashful about?" she chuckles, pinching his ear. "A man soon to turn thirty-seven who still blushes at the mention of a woman. Such a greenhorn!"

What could possibly be out there that Tiangou doesn't know about, he chortles under his breath at his doting auntie. Her words, however, leave him looking even more awkward. Tiangou is an innocent fellow, his aunt must know. But his effort backfires. She ceases her interrogation, sighing long and hard.

"Auntie," Tiangou can't resist asking, "is she as nice as, say, Wuxing's mother?" At that, he holds his breath.

"Not as gentle as Wuxing's mother, no, but she's much younger. You're naive about women, Tiangou. You aim to plant the biggest sweet potato, but when it comes to taking a wife, the younger, the more precious."

Tiangou still looks befuddled.

She pulls Tiangou over by the shoulder, spots a rip in his clothing and grabs a needle and thread. "That divorcée has a child," she says, beginning to stitch the tear, "which is not a bad thing. Her child isn't our own flesh and blood, but that doesn't mean that child won't look after us in our old age.

"I've mentioned you to her. She's not unwilling, but she said her elderly mother and a very young brother both rely on her support. If she is to remarry, some cash will need to go her family's way. So, how much savings do you have in hand?"

"Umm, three hundred or so," Tiangou replies. "A mere fly in a tiger's mouth!" exclaims she, "you need to save a bundle."

A chill stabs Tiangou in the heart. "If that's so, let's forget about it."

"Forget about what?" retorts auntie in that authoritative tone often voiced by seasoned folks. "Don't be naive! If you've never tasted candy, you don't know how sweet it can be. A wife is nice in oh so many ways: cooking you meals in the day, warming your feet at night, someone to chat with and keep you company. Best of all, she'll bear you sons and daughters and raise them. How can you remain half-hearted about this? Some time soon I'll take you for a quick once-over, and fix the engagement. As for the dowry, you can work on that at your own pace."

Three days later, Tiangou pays the woman a visit. Not as radiant as portrayed by his aunt, but she's still well-proportioned. When he relates the trip to Wuxing's mother, she is thrilled.

"Well, looks like it's finally going be settled then," says she. "Just grit your teeth and tighten your belt, Tiangou. Work harder the next few months and put aside every penny you can."

"It's just that the woman seems so, so calculated: She's not looking for a husband, she's hunting for somebody she can milk for money."

"Well, we womenfolk seldom see further than our nose, do we? But who can blame us, a woman has to weigh up everything and keep her feet on the ground."

"Not so with my Shi'niang!" protests Tiangou.

"Cheeky Tiangou!" she scolds him, chuckling.

Tiangou can be cheeky, that he admits. He's not one to fancify with sweet words, but he may blurt out something sour as a pickle, his teeth gleaming as he titters.

"How come I just don't hit it off with her?" he plows on, and his sober tone makes her look at him out of the corner of her eyes.

"So you turn your nose up at her because she's divorced?"

"No, I don't mind that. I'd be more than willing, Shi'niang, even if it was someone older, as long as she's kind!"

This remark alters her countenance dramatically. That was more than a slip of tongue, Tiangou quickly realizes. The air sizzles momentarily with awkwardness. Then she announces she's off to the hillside behind the village to cut and dry tasselgrass for kindling. Tiangou gets up to leave too.

"Tiangou," she calls as he steps outside, "come back just before dark. I'll roll some long noodles for you."

"Life's really getting better, eh? Long noodles for dinner?"

"Not just long noodles. Red-dyed eggs too! Take a wild guess: What day is tomorrow?"

It dawns on Tiangou — it's his very own birthday! "Shi'niang," says he, cheeks flushing, "Tiangou has no father or mother. You're the only one who remembers my birthday. How can Tiangou thank you enough!"

"Tut, tut, there goes cheeky Tiangou again. He's learned to grease his tongue!"

"Every word I say comes from the bottom of my heart," pleads Tiangou. "Just a word from you, Shi'niang, and Tiangou is content. I can live to be ninety-nine! As for celebrating my birthday, let's just forget it. Since I'm no longer Shifu's apprentice, why should you bother?"

"What? Your marriage is still hanging in midair, and already you're talking to me like I'm an outsider? This could well be the last birthday dinner I'll rustle up for you. When you're properly wedded, I'll save myself the trouble next year and show up at your door to enjoy the long noodles hand-rolled by your woman! No matter what, you have to come tonight. Your Threshold Year is coming to an end, and that's well worth celebrating!"

As she speaks, her eyes sparkle with a charm at once desired and dreaded by soft-hearted Tiangou. If he were made of ice, a mere glance from those eyes would melt him.

Tiangou returns home in great spirits. Standing beneath the eave, he gazes at the long-horned grasshoppers chirping in their tiny cages, and muses about Shi'niang's kindness. Warm and fuzzy, his thoughts glow:

Surely this woman is the reincarnation of a Bodhisattva? Each person enters the world to an end: A carpenter's purpose is to work wood and a mason's to shape rock; Shifu was born to bore wells, and Tiangou to put tasselgrass to good use; as for her, she must have come to this world purely to bequeath it with beauty and kindness ...

Tiangou is quite satisfied with his epiphanies, but then a new thought dawns: *The Bodhisattva, right now, is on her way to cut the coarse grass and dry it for fuel. Oh, those slender feet and tender hands, how much kindling can she reap? And why ain't I helping her right now?* Tiangou grabs his sickle and heads for the hillside.

The foot of the mountain is carpeted in grass. Towards the end of autumn, the blades have all turned champagne. Once it is ripe, the tasselgrass stiffens aureate with a heavy golden tinge, rustling in the wind. Tiangou stands amid the tussocks, craning his neck and looking about, but catches no glimpse of the woman. He bends down, slashing and hacking at a stretch, then binds the stalks into three bundles and stacks them together. When she arrives, he'll pop up from behind and give her a good fright.

But the Bodhisattva is nowhere in sight.

Tiangou carries his sickle down to a gully and hones it by a small spring. The puddle is shallow, and short blades of grass tremble in the ripples along its edges. A few centipedes glide on the water, rowing their multiple legs. Tiangou's hand is almost upon them, yet they remain perfectly composed; but just when he moves to snare one, the centipedes skim away like shadows.

He slashes the pool back and forth with the sickle, then slumps onto his back in the turf. Gazing into the speckless dome, he allows his thoughts to drift across the Scarlet River to the fair-skinned young divorcée, then back to a house where the Bodhisattva is making hand-rolled noodles, breasts bulging. His heart swells with glee, as if he were the Emperor enthroned in the Imperial Palace.

Over the past few years Tiangou has nourished a penchant for song, and melodies are now surging in his chest. He sets them free:

> *Missing my lass puts me on edge,*
>
> *A bunch of lampwick grass too heavy for carrying*
>
> *But hearing her voice from next door,*
>
> *Nine hills can I climb without tarrying.*

Each note lifts Tiangou's spirits higher than the last. *But who can hear my song?* Then the image of a certain someone surfaces, and he sings in her voice:

> *The lad yodels outside the gate,*
>
> *the lass weaving silk in her room.*
>
> *Why haven't you died of plague, O you sing so well!*
>
> *My legs are jelly, and my poor feet*
>
> *miss the Cloud Pedal, O your devilish songs!*

At the end of the song, Tiangou is tired. He glances down the path below, and someone is running towards him. Shi'niang, no doubt about it. But instead of standing up, he lays there and attempts to lure her over with his ditty. She spots him too, but stops abruptly.

"Tiangou! Tiangou!" she cries.

Something odd in her voice gets Tiangou up in a scramble.

"Come quick!" she blurts out, almost wailing, seeing his face. "Your Shifu has had an accident!"

Tiangou stops dead in mid-song, and his smile vanishes. He starts running down the hill toward her.

"What are you doing on the hillside? Couldn't find you anywhere!" she reproaches him. "Your Shifu was digging a well when it collapsed. He's stuck under a heavy rock and no one can pull him out. You've dug wells, Tiangou. Please, please come and save him. He was once your Master, after all!"

Whoosh! Tiangou hears the blood rushing into his brain. He wheels around and darts towards the village. But Shi'niang has collapsed behind him. He strides back, drags her to her feet, and with an arm around her, flies towards the Liu's house.

The courtyard is jam-packed. The well-digging here had penetrated eighty-three meters when a boulder blocked the way. The master digger had chiseled a hole in the monolith, filled it with explosives and set it off. He went down the narrow shaft again and found the rock had cracked. But he couldn't extricate the largest chunk, so he dug at it from the side. When the soil was cleared away, thinking the rock wouldn't budge, he began leveraging it with a crowbar. All of a sudden, the rock gave way and pinned him down from the waist.

The crowd above panicked. They sent someone down but no one dared pry the rock further, one shift and it could cost the trapped man his life. When the news reached Wuxing's mother, she ran pell-mell, yelling for her husband's former apprentice.

Without a moment's hesitation, Tiangou negotiates the passage downward. Legs lodged under the rock, the Master is in a coma. "Shifu, Shifu —!" Tiangou calls, pawing frantically at the soil beneath the unconscious man. Desperate and exhausted, he fears that any moment the rock will press down further if he isn't careful. With a monumental effort he finally pulls Shifu free, hoists the bloodied survivor on his back, and clambers to the mouth of the well.

After several days and nights of intense care, the well-digger is clawed back from the verge of death. But the nerves below his waist are beyond repair. The iron-willed craftsman is henceforth wasted, doomed to lie paralyzed on the earthen *kang* bed.

A peasant can lack for anything except for money, and can undergo anything, except for illness. For several years, Tiangou's Shifu bored wells like a true soldier, but when his career hit this low point, his household buckled like his legs.

For three months his wife waited at his bedside in the hospital, crying till her eyes were swollen and her mouth throbbed with blisters. Tiangou didn't have a chance to savor those longevity noodles for his birthday, and the kindling he bundled that afternoon was pilfered by some kids. He never returned to the hillside to dig up tasselgrass roots for whisk bristles, nor did he visit the provincial capital again to hawk them.

To seek a cure for Shifu, Tiangou carried him on his back to state-run hospitals accompanied by Shi'niang, and together they sought out famed country healers far and wide. Still, the well-digger cannot stand on his own two legs. In the end he is resigned, moaning like an aged ox on the bed and banging his head against the wall. A relentless flow of encouragement is kept up to talk the proud and ambitious man out of suicide. But his free fall into despondency seems to have damaged his brain, and most of the time he just appears absent.

These few grueling months cost the woman her former luster, leaving her haggard and frail. When she stands up after sitting on her heels doing chores, a dark mist envelops her vision. But even more torturous is watching the family savings trickling away like water. Despite their economic means being depleted day by day, she mustn't even raise her voice in front of her husband; all she can do is sob in a deserted corner.

Observing all this, Tiangou feels his own heart being pierced by a dagger. *If only I could swap places with Shifu! He possesses a lifelong talent, if only I could lie paralyzed on the* kang *in his stead, this family would be spared such torture!* Moreover, the sight of Shi'niang in such a pitiful state makes Tiangou more distressed than if it were him lying there motionless.

But Tiangou is not a member of this family, and his place is by the head of the *kang* counseling Shifu, or in the courtyard comforting Shi'niang. Aside from helping her tend the fields, feed the swine and clean the pigsty, he goes out looking for doctors and pays for the herbal concoctions out of his own pocket.

It takes an accident to completely transform a person. While the well-digger shed his despotic skin, his wife has grown tough. "When a man gets a woman, he matures," Tiangou used to proclaim. Yet with no companion at his side, Tiangou has somehow put on another ten years.

One day, Tiangou shows up again with a kilo of meat and a chunk of tofu in his hands.

"Tiangou," frowns Shi'niang, "I'll get angry if you keep this up! This household has turned into a bottomless black hole. Your savings will never fill it!"

"Don't you worry about it now, Shi'niang," replies Tiangou, "I'll get by one way or the other by myself."

"You're not sitting on a mountain of gold," she replies, "for some time now you haven't made a single brush to sell. Do you have some other skills up your sleeve? If you empty your pockets, what will be left to wed that woman across the river?"

Tiangou hasn't been up front with Shi'niang. The night before last, his aunt crossed the river bearing a message from the young woman. How was it going with the money, she wanted to know. "If you can't come up with one thousand *yuan* by month's end, then I'm done waiting. Quite a few moneyed bachelors have sent their matchmakers."

"Let that greedy woman sell herself to the highest bidder!" spat Tiangou. "A thousand bucks in my coffer? I could get ten plump porkers with that kind of money to bolster Shifu's health!"

This blunt comment earned him a fine dressing down. "Well, lad, do you still want a son or not?" rebuked his aunt.

"If I just put that sum aside, it'll at least lay me some copper sons!" barked Tiangou boorishly.

The old woman trembled ashen. The quarrel lasted the best part of the night before she stormed off.

"Tiangou," continues Shi'niang, ignorant of his squabble with his aunt, "the Country Fair is just around the corner on the third day of the third lunar month. All the young men are calling on their fathers-in-law. You'd better cross the river to visit her too, even though you aren't hitched yet.

"Anyhow, since you've bought the meat, let's not waste it. I'll also steam some buns tonight, so you can bring something to visit her tomorrow, ahead of the Country Fair."

The kind offer sets a wild bush fire in his heart. "I'm not going!" snaps Tiangou, completely forgetting that the Bodhisattva in front of him is trapped in suffering herself.

"How dare you!" she chides him.

Lying in the main room, the Master overhears everything and calls for Tiangou, banging the rim of his earthen *kang* bed. "How can you not go?" he asks as soon as Tiangou sets his foot inside. "You want to die alone and be a ghost remembered by no offspring?"

He pulls Tiangou by the hand to sit by his side. "Your Shifu is a useless lump now," he says, drawing a few breaths. "Ignore whatever I say as you like, but not this. Cross the river tomorrow, and make no fuss about it. Look at you, that coat is worse-worn than a painter's. Let your Shi'niang give it a good scrubbing tonight. Now go —!"

"But, but that woman brushed me off long ago!" admits Tiangou finally.

Not bothering with an explanation, he exits the room, strides straight across the courtyard and out the front gate.

For a brief moment, the well-digger and his wife are both dumbstruck. Then she begins to sob.

At night she goes to Tiangou's place and learns all the details. "What a sin!" she exclaims when it's clear that her family's misfortune is the undoing of Tiangou's courtship. She reprimands Tiangou for squandering his life's savings on her household.

"That low-lying bitch!" she curses, "all her eyes are on the money and she doesn't give a hoot who she's marrying!"

Though his name pops up every so often in her strong language, Tiangou only finds Shi'niang more virtuous and respectable. On and on she cusses, then she turns her ire on herself and can't stop weeping. Tiangou, meanwhile, stands there rooted like a child, at a loss where to put his hands or feet.

"Tiangou," she says between sobs, "we are the only ones to blame for this. It's a sin Wuxing's Father and I cannot atone for in this life. Now that things have come to this wretched end — our family is stone broke, and you stand no better off — even if you manage to put aside a few pennies, Tiangou, I won't allow you to waste it on us!

"Just look at our household: Money floods out but never seeps in, and we are cash-strapped in every corner. I've been thinking lately, maybe it's better to bring Wuxing back home and let him try his hand at something else!"

"Shi'niang," pleads Tiangou, "please don't. Wuxing missed several days of school last time, and it wasn't easy to get him back in class again. No matter how dire things get, his studies must not be disrupted."

About this, she understands only too well. Being a soft-hearted woman, she allows herself to be persuaded not to pull her son out of school. But the moment she catches sight of her husband's abject form, her heart turns the other way.

It's a turbulent night for the middle-aged couple. One moment they decide to end Wuxing's studies, agreeing that's the best option; the next moment they oppose the idea. Unable to relieve himself or wipe his own bottom, the well-digger breaks out in frustrated tears.

"I've dragged you and Wuxing down along with Tiangou," he says in between loud sniffling. "Damn it, why can't I just kick the bucket! Go get me a packet of rat poison and let me swallow it. At least I can save you some money on remedies!"

"Stop it, Wuxing's Father!" she begs, tears streaming down her cheeks. "Does anyone here ever look down on you? You're the backbone of this household, even if all you do is lie there and sleep. When you speak like that, you're just plunging a dagger in my heart. Do you think it's not already in pieces, my heart?"

Her man falls silent. Never before has the couple confided so much in each other, and their heart-to-heart helps them appreciate the other's warmth. The bitter twine of life has entangled the struggling pair of grasshoppers by the legs. Neither can bear to abandon the other.

The night grows old. The flame in the oil lamp crackles briefly in the niche on the wall, and then the oil is drained and the light fizzles out. She readies to light it again. "Leave it," says her husband. To save a match and a tad of lamp fuel, she lays him flat on his back, and two pairs of eyes glisten with tears in the dark night. Day by day his numb legs are shriveling, his wife massages them under the quilt to stimulate circulation. Grappling with his legs, she turns him over a few times, then strips naked and snuggles up by her man like a kitten before falling asleep.

In the small hours of the night, she wakes up in a shudder and finds her husband gently nudging her. "Trouble sleeping?" she murmurs.

"Didn't catch a wink. I've got something to tell you."

She sits up, gathers the quilt over her shoulders and touches a wet corner. It is soaked in his tears. Through the latticed window comes dim moonlight, barely enough for her to see his grief-torn visage.

"All my life I've been fighting to take first place," he begins, "and I was damn full of myself. For nearly two decades we've been man and wife, but I never treated you properly. Just the thought of it fills my heart with remorse.

"I'm done for. I won't get out of this bed until my dying day. 'The sick over-think,' they always say, and I've been lying here thinking, day and night, about everything, my final moment in particular. You told me off and you were right to do so. I'm too ashamed to die; I reckon I'll just hang on. But this household of ours, we can't let it continue like this forever, Wuxing's Mother!

"And so I've been thinking, you know, you don't have to leave me, and I, I'll still be your man. But it's always been the man who provides for his woman in this world. How can a man live off his wife?

"In the North and South Mountains, you see, there are those who 'marry anew to support the old' ..."

She remains perfectly still, a clutch of fear gripping her throat more tightly with each word he utters. In the end, she reaches out and covers his mouth.

"Stop," she says in a quavering voice. "I'm not listening to this. What horrible thoughts have wormed into your head while you lie here!" Dollops of tears drop onto the already damp quilt.

Getting married again in order to support an existing husband — such customs do still linger deep in the mountains. This Bodhisattva of a woman has heard tell of such things, but that was nothing more than gossip, something to spice up the conversation. Now, her very own husband is begging her to play a role in such a drama! She shakes from head to toe like grain being winnowed to separate it from the chaff.

Her misery makes her husband feel his own heart and guts are being wrenched and shredded. "As a man it's shameful for me to bring it up," he concedes, sighing deeply. "But you won't let me die or follow my suggestion, you are condemning me to lie here watching you suffer, yet unable to lift a finger. Even if I don't die by rope or poison, my aching heart alone will snuff me out twice over!"

"I'd do anything if it's for you," she wails, throwing herself onto his heaving chest. "But it's a new husband you are asking me to find! Where shall I even begin? What single man in his right mind would set foot in our door? And even if someone does come, it might be bearable if he's decent; if he treats you like dirt, I'd cry my eyes dry!"

Locked in one another's arms, the couple cries until daybreak. At dawn, wolf howls come from the mountains far behind the village, as if someone were moaning in agony.

Early in the morning, she heads again for the hillside behind the village to cut grass and dry it for kindling. "Go to the sunny slope," advises her husband, "never go down to the shady dell. If you spot something that looks like a dog, first cry 'Wolf! WOLF!' Don't fall for that beast playing a dog. And if it happens that you startle some wasps, never ever run. Just cover your hair and face in grass, and play dead on the spot ..."

His wife repeats twice to herself everything he said, and sets out. As soon as her footsteps fade, the well-digger breaks into a heart-wrenching howl. In no time flat, an alarmed neighbor races in.

"Please," urges the invalid, "please bring me Tiangou. I've something really important to tell him."

Meanwhile, Tiangou has been cooped up at his home, sulking. Whatever he picks up refuses to take shape in his fingers, and out of boredom he succumbs to braiding a grasshopper cage. It's just the third month after the Spring Festival, and long-horned grasshoppers aren't active yet. With no chirping to relieve his troubled thoughts, Tiangou gazes vacantly at the empty cage.

By the time he reaches Shifu's side, Tiangou is prepared lest the topic of Wuxing abandoning school come up. "Shifu," says he reassuringly, "as long as Tiangou remains standing, I am forever your disciple. I am a 'Celestial Dog,' true to my name, not a mongrel that bites the hand that feeds it. True, this 'Celestial Dog' may not amount to much, but Tiangou will fight tooth and nail to keep Shifu's family above water. We must not distract Wuxing from his books, no matter what."

"I must have been blind as a bat, Tiangou, to kick you out of the well," says his former Master. "Good for nothing, every man is. Only when disasters befall him does he come to his senses, but by then it is too late.

Now, be honest with your Shifu: That woman across the river, is she really a lost cause?"

"She's history," admits Tiangou, "that sort of woman is born with itchy palms! Put aside the fact that she's unwilling to marry the likes of me, given her behavior, if she were a maiden of just over seventeen and blooming like a dainty flower, I'd just stomp right over, pick up a tile, dump it on her head, then go on my way and never once look over my shoulder. Just think about it, if Shi'niang were even remotely like that wench, she'd have walked out on you ages ago."

"Indeed," sighs the Master, "your Shi'niang is such a dove, putting up with my quick temper ever since we married. A golden heart, that woman surely has. Having chanced upon a wife like this, I, Li Zheng, ought to be content with whatever life throws my way.

"But she's suffering too much these days. She's just a frail woman, after all, and there's no labor in the fields, or any helping hand inside the home or out. If we don't take Wuxing out of school, who's there to help prepare the food and drink and foot the bill for everything else, and wipe the arse of an invalid on top of that? The very thought makes my heart shatter.

"I've been thinking, Tiangou, there is a path she can take: 'Marry anew to support the old.' Tell me from the bottom of your heart, would that work?"

Tiangou's heart throbs with pain. *His crippled state has transformed Shifu into someone else. To reach this decision, how his heart must have bled! No, no,* Tiangou tells himself, shaking his head. *But, if she doesn't take this path, my poor Shi'niang may never escape the Sea of Suffering.* Again his head begins to shake. The lack of power to undo what Heaven has ordained leaves Tiangou indecisive. For a long while, neither speaks.

"Shifu," says he in the end, "have you talked this over with Shi'niang?"

"She won't listen to reason," says he, "but mine is the best option, if we're being honest with ourselves. We wouldn't be breaking any laws, or turn ourselves into a laughing stock. What do you say?"

"Then," asks Tiangou tentatively, "do you have someone in mind?"

No reply comes. His Master is visibly struggling. In the end he pulls his ex-apprentice over. "It's next to impossible, Tiangou," he begins, "who'd come to our place? If I so much as mention one word of it, your Shi'niang dissolves in tears.

"What I have in mind is, by now you must know your Shi'niang by heart and soul, there are less than a handful in this whole village who can claim themselves her equal. She's going on forty, there's no denying it, but you can't tell from her looks ..." His voice trails off, but his eyes are glued to Tiangou's.

Tiangou, no fool, has heard what his Master didn't say. His heart skips a beat, and he suddenly becomes interested in his feet.

Once again, silence floods the room. Tiangou slips down the *kang* and slumps onto the circular straw mat.

Outside, a huge pile of branches enters the courtyard. Shi'niang is bent double under a basket on her back piled high with branches. "*Thud*!" she unloads her burden at the southeastern corner of the wall, where firewood and grass for kindling are stacked haphazardly into a sizeable hill. Strands of soaked hair stuck on her forehead, she is just sitting down to catch her breath when Tiangou emerges.

"Tiangou!" she calls.

Eyes glazed, Tiangou marches straight out the gate without glancing back.

Commencing on the third day of the third lunar month, for three days the fortified village perched on the bank of the Scarlet River is immersed in the Country Fair's festivities. Peasants cease their labor, enjoying themselves at home or calling on their relatives and friends nonstop.

Brightly dressed up for the occasion, the betrothed men visit their future parents-in-law — "Mount Tai" and "River Tai" — with four types of fine offerings. Mount Tai and River Tai also take this occasion to show their generosity for the first time by permitting their daughter to join her young fiancé in gathering wild fern in the mountains. The rich rain that comes with the third lunar month has nurtured the bracken fern so well that sap drips off the tender shoots upon the lightest touch. In a glen behind a cliff, amidst a thicket of Red-Eyed Cat, the fern-gatherers also harvest the fruit of love, juicy and ripe.

The back window of Tiangou's house opens to the mountains. Admiring the framed landscape tableau, he quietly intones the lyrics he used to sing for this rural festival:

Chubby'n'short there goes my darling,
on her back an oblong basket.
For fern in the hill she is coming,
with a sharp eye out for her beau,
O so much has she her love to tell!

At the end of the song, Tiangou sighs deeply. Then he pulls the window shut, throws himself onto the *kang*, covers his head with the quilt and tries to get some shuteye. Never before has he been so listless. He doesn't wish to encounter anyone, so it is after all are sound asleep that he finally emerges.

Soon he finds himself at the wall enclosing the village and sits on the stone slab at the entry into the passageway. This is the second time he has come down here deep at night, and the familiar scenery triggers a jumbled mix of feelings. In the distance, the Scarlet River's shoal shimmers white, not a sound hails from that direction. There is no eclipse tonight, and the moon is not the one to be devoured by the fabled Celestial Dog. But here on earth, the mythical canine's namesake, already thirty-seven and still a virgin, is besieged by troubled thoughts.

Via Shi'niang —at once his Master's wife, Tiangou's Moon and a Bodhisattva — Tiangou has come to understand the meaning of a real woman. Throughout the year he served as Shifu's apprentice, and in the dozen years he has lived as Shi'niang's neighbor in the same village, Tiangou has long nursed a soft spot for this woman. A twist of her waist, her gait, or a glance from those eyes that speak never fail to electrify his body. And he savors those charged moments for hundreds, no, thousands of times, lest they fade into oblivion.

Tiangou has doubted and even dreaded these feelings. *You should never harbor such improper thoughts,* he admonishes himself time and again. But surprising even himself, he finds only pure love in his heart for this woman, and each loving impulse has kept any racy whim at bay. Tiangou is certainly no sage, but if he does feel shame before this woman, and is able to rein himself in, surely that would rank him among the virtuous? And so Tiangou emboldens himself to regard this affection, even love, as a need essential to his very life, and he assumes the demeanor of a child, shy and obedient before his Bodhisattva, basking in her favor.

On that night of lunar eclipse, it was right here that she sang a song to bring back the moon and prayed for the safety of her husband, and a younger man too. That night, Tiangou also sang two ballads just for her. *If songs had souls, would they inhabit the river,* he wonders, *or the grass?*

And now, should I become her second husband?

The one who brought this up was not Tiangou, nor his beloved Shi'niang, but his very own Shifu, her true lawful husband! And how should he reply? "I'm willing, and I've always wanted to!" That's what Tiangou ought to say, but he just cannot bring himself to utter those words. She is Shi'niang — a motherly figure Tiangou venerates and depends upon — and who is he to boldly proclaim, "I am her man!" ?

Tiangou, Tiangou, where have your wits and bravery gone? His face scarlet as if covered in red cloth, he dares not steal a glance at Shifu, Shi'niang, or even himself. Whether he's facing the mirror in the house, the water deep in the well, or the moon that shines exceptionally bright tonight, no, he dares not look — *might Tiangou be that colossal monster, after all?*

The fourth day is Sunday.

Wuxing, freshly back from school, goes to the sandy banks along the river to scavenge licorice root.

"Wuxing," greets Tiangou when he spots the boy, "what are you digging for?"

"Herbal medicine for my Mum," replies the boy.

"Oh?" panics Tiangou, "is your mother ill?"

"I came back from school," relates Wuxing, "and my parents had an argument. Mum took to bed and said her tummy's swollen and her heart aches. So Dad sent me down here."

A dizzy spell sweeps over Tiangou as he stands uncertainly on the sandy shoal.

"Uncle Tiangou, are you alright?"

"Umm, the sun's a bit hot today. How about your studies, Wuxing, making good progress?"

"Mum told me not to go anymore, Uncle Tiangou."

"Didn't we persuade her not to stop your studies?"

"But it's Mum who said it, and she said it down on her knees: 'Things are tough for the family these days, we mustn't burden your Uncle Tiangou like this.' And she told me to come home to work."

Tiangou bites his tongue and returns home, where he bursts out crying. He packs his things, determined to leave the village unnoticed for the provincial capital. Like a cloud that holds no promise of rain, a swathe of free-flowing water, he must exile himself beyond the horizon.

And yet his feet refuse to obey. Leading to the entrance of the wall encircling the village are three hundred and seventy-two stone steps. He descends three hundred stairs only to retrace two hundred. At this moment, Tiangou is an agitated lion in a zoo pacing back and forth in its cage, a generalissimo in a movie poring over maps on the eve of the final battle.

Eventually, Tiangou makes it to the gate of his Master's house.

"Shi'niang," he announces, "I'm here. I'll do as Shifu says!"

Rinsing rice by the door, the woman freezes under the sudden shock, unable to feel or perceive, devoid of desire or thought, as rice trickles through her fingers like sand. Suddenly her face contorts and hot tears gush forth.

"Tiangou!" she cries and

rushes through the doorway, only to collapse in a heap on the threshold where she weeps in silence, unable to utter a single syllable.

The village officials, clan elders, and a clerk from the township government one-and-a-half-mile away gather at the well-digger's for drinks on the *kang*. Face to face, the delegates acknowledge this unique union and approve the trio's atypical family. Once three fingers have each pressed a crimson print on a thick sheet of paper, the bedridden man requests that he be propped up by a quilt, and then he toasts the guests, Tiangou, the woman, and himself to boot. "*Glug glug,*" down goes the liquor in one go.

For three days Wuxing plays truant, then he heads out for school once again — a firm request on the part of his new Father. Tiangou insists on sending the boy off and only stops after six miles.

"Father," says Wuxing, "please return home now."

"Say 'Uncle'," insists Tiangou.

"Uncle," the boy obeys promptly, winning a genial smile from Tiangou.

In local courtyards, the dinner table is normally set in the center of the main room. At the well-digger's, a short-legged table is placed atop the *kang*. It was set there before, and remains so. While the two men sit on opposite sides of the table, the woman doesn't take a seat; she eats in front of the earthen stove, where kindling is thrust beneath the wok, and the heat is channelled into the *kang* next to the stove in winter. As soon as she spots an emptied bowl she retrieves it with both hands, and returns it filled, still with both hands.

It is time to irrigate the wheat, and day and night the peasants are toiling in the fields, bent over double. No longer do they eat together. The woman makes sure that a poached egg lies in the bowl for her senior husband at each meal. But he never touches it and quietly stashes the egg at the bottom of the second bowl. When Tiangou comes home later, he sits by Shifu and begins to eat.

"Oh? There's a worm in the

rice," he remarks to the woman perched by the stove, and deposits his bowl on the oven top. When she comes to finish his leftovers, there is no worm to be found; it has morphed into an egg.

As the meals gradually improve, all three faces take on a healthy florid complexion.

On that day before the delegates gathered at their house to drink at night, the well-digger had dispatched the woman to prepare the stand-alone hut next to the main dwelling. That afternoon she pasted new wallpaper on the ceiling, swept the dust, and laid out the bedding. She was to spend the night there, instructed her husband. But she refused.

Before nightfall, the well-digger cast the pillow embroidered with a pair of loving mandarin ducks out the window, and wrapped himself in the quilt to sleep alone on the *kang*. When she retrieved the pillow, he grabbed the stick propping up the window and beat the bed rim like a madman.

Frightened witless, she scurried to the hut to rest, but left the door unbolted. Early in the evening during the first *geng*, she heard dogs barking and got up to close the door; two hours later at the second *geng*, someone walked by their courtyard, so she got up again and undid the latch inside the door before lying down, eyes wide open; in the quiet of midnight, only crickets were heard chirping by the wall; she drifted off briefly in the wee hours of the fourth *geng*; when the fifth *geng* arrived before dawn, silent tears were falling thick and fast, a corner of the quilt clenched in her teeth.

That night, Tiangou never showed.

Once upon a time,
Tiangou was tough'n'-mighty
like a tiger, day'n'night
gallant as a soldier.
Since he entered the house,
he's shy today, forlorn on the morrow,
a weeping shriveled candle,
his head ne'er again held high.

Once upon a time,

the woman had few words and
a steady gaze, her mind
a straight line that never strays.
Since he entered the house,
she's forlorn today, shy on the morrow,
a broken gate never shut
tightly by night or by day.

And thus time sails by uneventfully, with everyone reticent and restrained. While an old day never overstays its welcome, the next ushers in new anxieties.

At the end of another dinner, the two men sit on the *kang*, puffing away at their pipes, raindrops pitter-pattering outside. In two hours of rain, the last bit of tobacco powder in the pouch has turned to smoke and ashes. Tiangou gets up and reaches for the straw rain-cape hanging on the column.

"Tiangou, you ..." begins his elder.

"It's getting late, you should rest," says Tiangou, as if not cottoning on. "It'll rain again early tomorrow morning. I've arranged for an amateur folk opera group to come and liven things up in our household."

This sets off his Shifu. "*Thunk*!" he bangs the wooden window prop against the edge of the *kang*. "You do that," he bellows, "and I'll drop dead right in front of you!"

Tiangou stands there rigid as a column. "Shifu ..." he says, full of a son's reverence. Then he turns and walks out in silence.

Outside, the rain pelts down even harder.

1986

The Brick Bed

By Jia Pingwa
Translated by Denis Mair

She was a matron who lived in Yang'ergou in north Shaanxi Province, eighty *li* to the east of the county seat and thirty *li* to the west of Suoguan Town. In her whole life she never went to the county seat — so she had no idea how thick the ramparts could be — and only four times to Suoguan Town. Each time she went to the temple fair on the first day of each month, but after coming home her feet would ache for days. She had once hated her mother for binding her feet as a child; what is more, she vowed that in the next life she would not be born as a woman, unable to travel boldly across the land.

Her birth family had lived on the central Shaanxi Plain, but at age 19 a relative had acted as a go-between and married her off to a family here. Her husband's surname was Wang; he was three years her junior and monkey-like in stature. With a bout of crying she made her unwillingness known, but her parents had already accepted the Wangs' money, so her protests were futile: she had no choice but to climb onto Wang's bed and become a wife. On the day set for receiving the bride, her husband came to pick her up on a donkey. Four *suona* players tootled and filled the air with blaring notes as villagers lined the road to view the festivities. She timidly clutched the donkey's back, not daring to look up. That evening, after the groom's friends finished the horseplay in the nuptial chamber, the door of the cave-house was closed behind them, leaving her alone with Monkey-Face. Pangs of separation from her mother triggered another fit of sobbing, so her husband dared not touch her that night. On the third night, Monkey-Face crawled across the bed to her and addressed her "Housewife." She said, "I am not your housewife. Call me 'Sister'!" Her husband called her Sister, and only then did she give him a smile.

Being a wife felt quite different from being an unmarried girl. Her husband could not shield her from rain and wind, but he was devoted and affectionate, so she gave in. He sometimes led a string of pack mules to Dingbian, hauling salt for one or two months each time, during which she kept busy with indoor and outdoor work at home: in the winter she planted wheat; in the summer she sowed millet. If she had free time she would visit neighbors chattering while doing some needlework. As time went by she came around to the view that this place was not bad, especially that heated brick bed. She had never seen a bed like that on the central Shaanxi Plain, so she found it intriguing.

The brick bed was big, measuring approximately three and a half meters in length and two and a quarter meters in width. It took up half of the whole cave-house. Beneath the cave's front window was a stove that had a deep cavity on top where charcoal was added. The fire was used for cooking meals, and it was connected to the brick bed by a duct underfoot. In winter the cave-house stayed warm, but she was not used to such a big bed. The first time her husband went away, she wrapped herself in a big cover and had the whole bed to herself at night. She rolled this way and that during the night, making herself chuckle a few times. She suggested that he re-do the brickwork to make the bed smaller, but he didn't agree, claiming that when they had children in the future, the bed would be able to sleep eight or ten people. Hearing him say this made her face blush. Getting up at night to use the chamber-pot, she would always think: if we really do have seven or eight kids, their shoes will make a long row beneath the bed. That made her chuckle again.

The brick bed became her personal domain: she sat on it while spinning yarn and sewing cloth shoes; on its broad surface she spread her bundle of possessions; in her idle time she would sort through colorful silk threads and pieces of cloth. In the evening, she and her husband would murmur confidences there. She thought: a man makes his way freely through the outside world; a woman should watch over this brick bed. She did her best to make it look nice, spreading the covers without a wrinkle and not letting a speck of dust settle along its base. Even so she could not get in the habit of eating on the bed, saying that was hard on her legs.

Three years later she still hadn't given birth, not even to a daughter. Although her husband was vexed, he could not bring himself to speak harshly to her. She went off by herself and cried miserably over her cruel fate. After that, feeling a little guilty, she never tried to get the upper hand over her husband, and he ended up showing more love and affection for her.

By this time the Central Red Army had arrived at Yan'an after the Long March and had liberated several counties along the northwest border. Even so, General Hu Zongnan's White Army often made forays, so a see-saw conflict unfolded across this piece of terrain. During those unquiet times, the Whites would come, and then the Reds would drive them away. That day, gunfire was heard for two hours, coming from the southeast, so the villagers stayed behind closed doors. As darkness fell and they barred the door, preparing to sleep, they heard the thud of something landing in the yard outside the cave. Going out for a look, they found a female soldier of the Eighth Route Army. She told them that her unit had scattered in the face of a fierce onslaught, and she had gotten separated from her squad.

She asked to come inside the cave and rest. This gave the wife a fright, but she let the woman soldier come inside.

The soldier's face was a waxy yellow, and her protuberant torso moved stiffly. The wife could tell at a glance that the female soldier was pregnant, which made her all the more solicitous. She boiled water and told the female soldier to sit on the bed. Seeing the couple's kindness, the female soldier was quite grateful, but after all they were a newly married couple occupying a single cave, so staying there did not seem convenient. The husband was indecisive, but the wife said, "Get up on the bed. This is our custom here in North Shaanxi — people under the same roof sleep on the same *kang*."

She told the female soldier to sleep on the west side and her husband to sleep on the east, with herself in the middle as a barrier. Still the female soldier would not go to sleep. The wife had no choice but to rouse her husband and make him stretch out on the ground in front of the stove, saying he was only allowed to face outward. Her husband laid there all night without daring to turn over.

At night she asked the female soldier in a hushed tone: "How many years have you been a soldier?"

"One year and eight months."

"Have you killed anyone?"

"I had a White soldier in my sights and pulled the trigger. He fell down and didn't get up, but I didn't stick around to see if he was dead."

"You really have what it takes. My hands get quivery just from killing a chicken."

"It was forced upon me. My father and mother were bayoneted by the White army; then I was sold by my clan to another family as a child bride, but I ran away."

She felt a twitch in her heart and unconsciously directed a look at her husband.

"Where is your husband now?"

"He is in Yan'an. Right now he may be off somewhere fighting a battle."

"How far along is your pregnancy?"

"Seven-and-a-half months."

"Good grief. It's horrible to be running about in your condition."

"I really regret getting pregnant. If only I could get it ripped out of me!"

The next day, the female soldier got ready to go. The wife held her back, saying it would be terrible if the birth happened along the way. So the female soldier agreed to stay in the cave. The wife found out the woman's name — it was Gong Juan, and she was a propaganda staffer.

That night, Gong Juan felt pain in her belly, and the pain began coming in spasms. The wife roused her husband from his slumber at the base of the bed, telling him to bring in a bundle of straw. Then she locked him outside the cave. Neither of the women had dealt with a birth before, so they fumbled about with trembling hands. After an ordeal of almost ten hours, the child finally came into the world onto the straw. The wife strewed ashes over the bloodied foot-platform, then called her husband in. She cooked a meal and heated the bed, then hung a red streamer in the doorway, saying it would ward off ill fortune.

The child was a girl, as skinny as a cat, so they called her Kitty. Gong Juan was delighted with her, and so were the husband and wife. They kept the cave door closed all day, not letting any word of the child slip out. After ten days of sitting on the brick bed, Gong Juan grew restless, wanting to go and find her squad. Before leaving she set Kitty on the bed and knelt in front of the wife, saying: "Elder-Sister, I cannot stay any longer. I can't take this child with me, so I'm leaving her in your care. Let's just say you will be her lifesaver. If she turns out well, then you can raise her up and have her for a daughter. If something is wrong with her, then bury her. Either way, I'll owe you a lifelong debt for your kindness."

The wife helped Gong Juan to her feet and said tearfully: "Sister Gong, you can go with your mind at ease. Though I live in a poor household, my conscience is still intact. Your child is my child; I will bring it up as best I can. When peaceful days come again, I'll wait for you to come and get her back."

Gong Juan prostrated herself before the wife, touching her forehead to the floor several times. She held the child, kissing it and sobbing. When she had cried enough, she left.

On this brick bed the wife began to raise the child Kitty. She had no milk and the child was squalling with hunger. She told her husband to sell the new quilt from their bed, with which he bought a milch goat. Each day they milked the goat to feed the child. She let out word that she had picked up a foundling beside the road and, being unable to conceive a child herself, she had decided to raise it. No one in the village doubted her. Two years passed: she still did not bear a child of her own. Gong Juan still did not come for the child, which led the wife to believe that she had fallen in battle. It also made the wife's affection for the child grow all the stronger.

When Kitty was three years old, the monkeyish husband contracted tuberculosis. Her attempts to nurse him through the fever failed, and he passed away. She had a good long cry, and after that she would not remarry. She became a widow at the age of twenty-six.

As a widow times were even harder than before. She became a woman of few words, and she did not lightly go out her gate. At times wild dogs or feral cats would come near; she would chase them out of the cave and close the door. Among her neighbors there were no gossips about her.

She was stoical, with high self-esteem, able to hide the most grievous hardships within herself, and never showing the slightest anxiety in front of others. Although Kitty's clothes were somewhat drab, they were absolutely clean. For all household expenses she relied on her spinning work. She spun thread and yarn, rapidly and neatly: other people could only spin one cattie three ounces per day, but she could spin two catties one ounce. The thread she spun brought a better price than the thread spun by others.

In spring of that year the Northwest was thoroughly liberated, and more people in the village were spinning thread than before. The government began purchasing cotton thread and wool yarn. From then on she never sold her thread for a high price in the market; she reserved it to sell to the government. When the local cadres praised her at an assembly, she announced Kitty's parentage, saying: "The child's mother was an enlisted woman in the Eighth Route Army, a woman who went up against the enemy with gun in hand. I have to spin as much thread as I can to be a worthy foster mother for Kitty." The village selected her and a man named Wu Erzhang to take part in a "Model Worker Assembly" in Yan'an, but ultimately she did not go. She felt that being a woman was her lot in life, and it wouldn't be fitting to show off in front of many people. Whether or not she was recognized as a model worker, she would try to spin more thread anyway. As for Wu Erzhang, having been named a model worker he was recruited to fight in Shanxi. He won a combat medal, and after the founding of New China in 1949 served as a cadre in Xi'an. Meanwhile she went on living in Yang'ergou, spinning cotton thread night and day on her brick bed.

After the founding of New China, Kitty grew to girlhood. The woman paid for Kitty's schooling, and Kitty's excellence as a student reflected well on her. Lying on the brick bed arm-in-arm with Kitty she said, "Do you love me?"

"Yes."

"When you grow up will you support me?"

"Yes, I will."

She hugged Kitty tightly.

But that fall as she stood in her courtyard knocking down jujubes with a long pole, she heard an automobile engine. Looking up she saw a sedan pulling up at the edge of the road. A group of city folks tumbled out of the car and came walking straight toward her cave-house. It was quite an unusual sight, and she had no idea who the people were. She was telling Kitty that it was called an "automobile" when the group walked into her yard. Among them, a city woman in her late thirties spoke the greeting "Big Sister," then burst out crying. It was baffling at first, until the woman identified herself as Gong Juan. "*Oh*, you're still alive!" she exclaimed and began sobbing too.

That night they stayed up talking until dawn. Gong Juan told how she had gone out from the cave and found her unit. Before long they advanced to the front line. After that she was sent to Xinjiang, and she never made it back to northern Shaanxi. After the founding of New China, she tried to make inquiries, but no answer came. The news had come to her only a month ago.

"Big Sister, I know it hasn't been easy for you. You wiped her butt and kept her well-fed through babyhood, so she could grow into a girl. Really, I don't know how to show my gratitude. Now the revolution has succeeded. I can hardly bring myself to take her away and leave you here alone. I'll tell you what, you can come to the city with us. I will always call you Older Sister, and Kitty will always call you Mother."

The village woman laughed, saying she had done nothing to be worthy of going to the city. She urged Kitty to recognize the city woman as birth-mother. At first Kitty didn't want to go to the city, so the village woman put on a stern face.

The next day she smilingly saw off the girl and Gong Juan, but when the car was out of sight she fell over on the road and wailed wretchedly.

Now that she had a relative in Xi'an City, every few days she would ask someone to write a letter for her, and she received answering letters from the mother and daughter. She occasionally received small sums of money from them, eight or ten *yuan* at a time. She couldn't bear to spend it on herself, so she bought local produce and mailed it. They invited her to make a trip to the city, just for fun. In one letter she agreed to go, but she never got around to it.

After Kitty graduated from middle school, Gong Juan contracted an illness and died. Not long after that, Kitty began a full-time job, and fewer letters came. First there were two letters each month, but later once in half a year. The letters that did come were shorter and shorter, and eventually no word came at all.

Even so she kept waiting expectantly. Every third day or so she inquired at the post office. People in the village felt sorry for her and said, "We've heard that Kitty was promoted to bureau chief."

"Is that so?"

"I wonder if she has a conscience. Now that she's an official, she forgets you!"

"That is no way to talk. Serving as a leader keeps her busy."

"Even if she's busy it's not right to forget you. You raised her. I think she owes it to you to provide for you."

"If I raised her back then just so she would support me now, what kind of person would I be?"

She said this for other people to hear, but also for herself to hear. Thus she was able to take a broad view and didn't hold anything against Kitty. She just kept spinning cotton yarn; she spun from spring to summer and then from summer to winter. Half of the money she earned went for new clothes and half went for staple foods. If anyone broached the subject of Kitty, she would smooth her new jacket and tap the edge of her bowl, saying, "Talking about that doesn't get us anywhere. I'm not an old lady in my seventies or eighties; I'm getting by, aren't I?"

Yet the big brick bed was mighty hard to sleep on, so she put down padding of straw all through the year. People advised her to take out the bed and have a smaller one made. She wouldn't do it. She said that she could let go of everything else, but not that brick bed. Sleeping on that brick bed, she could have plenty of dreams—about her monkeyish husband or about Kitty and her mother.

During those years, cadres from county and provincial governments were frequently sent down to the countryside. Many of them were men, but women also came. When female cadres came, the village would arrange for them to sleep on the woman's brick bed. She was glad to let eight or ten of them squeeze onto the brick bed. She stayed up later than them, and as she held the lamp she could see a line of pretty faces. Looking down she saw their shoes placed along the base of the bed, which reminded her of a conversation with her husband years before. She held back a laugh as she arranged the varicolored shoes in a neat row. In the morning the female cadres brushed their teeth while she rinsed her mouth with salt water. Her teeth were not as straight as before but were still white like jade.

Around the time she turned sixty, the Great Proletarian Cultural Revolution broke out, and fewer female cadres came to sleep on her brick bed. She often thought of them and could remember all their names. Yet she never spoke of Kitty in front of them. When the jujubes in her yard turned ripe and red, she would sometimes think of Kitty, deep in her heart, and feel sad for a spell.

A couple of years passed, and peace was not yet restored in society, when groups of students started coming to the countryside from Beijing, Nanjing and Xining. They had to join production brigades and settle down in the village. She discretely inquired about Kitty: some of the students knew about Kitty: they said she had been branded as a "capitalist roader" and had been paraded through the streets with her head shaven. Hearing this made the woman's heart ache: while caring for Kitty as a child she had never laid a finger on the girl. How could Kitty bear such mistreatment?

Suddenly one day the postman brought a letter. This gave the woman a terrible start, because she did not know who would write to her. Only when it was read to her did she know it was from Kitty. It was a heartbreaking letter that told how Kitty had committed errors and was now being reformed at a cadre education farm. Kitty already had three children of her own, and people were prejudiced against them. Preparations were underway to send the children to a remote area. Kitty was worried about them and was hoping to send her oldest daughter to live in Yang'ergou under the woman's care. Kitty admitted to forgetting her roots and not keeping in touch with her own foster mother, so she feared the woman would not be willing.

The woman's tears poured down as she heard the letter being read. She quickly asked someone to write a return letter, which went as follows:

"Let her come! Let her come! Why should I be unwilling? Since the child has difficulties, have her come here and she can live in my place. I still have that big brick bed. The girl will keep me company, and nobody will dare to mistreat her. Let her come soon!"

Before long Kitty's oldest daughter arrived, a sixteen-year-old girl named Xiuxiu, with eyes that looked much like Kitty's. At first sight Xiuxiu called the woman "Grandma." The woman inadvertently called out "Kitty" and embraced her tearfully.

So then Xiuxiu was there with her. Lying in bed each night, she told Xiuxiu stories about Kitty's childhood which provoked both into a chuckle at times. Xiuxiu for her part spoke of what her family had gone through for the past few years. Xiuxiu's story reduced her to tears and kept her awake half the night.

Xiuxiu did not know how to do anything. The woman taught her to recognize food crops, use a hoe and wash clothes. She admonished the girl to be upright in character and not to shrink from doing hard work. Xiuxiu was a well-behaved girl and did as she was told. Coming home from work and seeing that the woman had supper ready, Xiuxiu would scoop the first portion into the woman's bowl. The woman's hands trembled with joy to see such thoughtfulness. At winter's end Xiuxiu began having her monthly periods. At first Xiuxiu was scared and didn't know what to do. The woman took her in hand and gave her pointers, telling her not to touch cold water and not to do heavy work. One night menstrual cramps and separation from her mother caused Xiuxiu to lie awake crying. The woman stayed up all night urging Xiuxiu to look at the bright side. Seeing that the woman was so protective of Xiuxiu, no one in the village dared to treat the girl harshly.

After a stay of two years,

Xiuxiu had grown into an attractive young woman with broad shoulders and firm, pert breasts. During that period Xiuxiu made three short visits to Xi'an, and each time Kitty would send along clothes to give the woman.

The woman asked Xiuxiu, "Which do you like more, the countryside or the city?"

"I like the countryside."

"In the future if your mother gets tired of living in the city, have her come here to live."

"That would be nice. I would watch over you all my life."

"Then someday we'll find a son-in-law who's willing to marry into our household."

"But where would he live?"

"There's plenty of room for a young couple to sleep on such a large bed."

"Heehee..." Xiuxiu's blushing face looked like a flower.

At the end of spring Xiuxiu went back to the city. The woman asked Xiuxiu to relay a message to Kitty, saying Kitty's whole family could come to the village and live in the countryside. No one in the village would dare to shave Kitty's head and parade her on the streets. A month passed after Xiuxiu left, but still she did not come back. The woman was anxious, fearing that something had happened to Xiuxiu along the way, so she sent a cable to the city. Before long a letter came in return.

The letter was from Xiuxiu, saying that her mother had been vindicated and had regained her post as bureau chief. Now they would be able to have Xiuxiu's sent-down sisters transferred back to the city.

"But I still want to return to Yang'ergou," continued Xiuxiu's letter. "I don't feel right leaving you, and I'm used to sleeping on that heated brick bed. I can't get to sleep on a thick mattress, in an upstairs room, but I can't get to sleep."

The woman was greatly relieved, but at the same time was on pins and needles. She worried that something might prevent Xiuxiu from coming. All the villagers were saying, "Xiuxiu won't be coming back. She probably found a job in the city, so it's not likely she'd be back and suffer here." Each time the woman would reply, "Xiuxiu says she'll come back. She says the brick bed suits her."

As it turned out, Xiuxiu did not come back, but she did send four letters. Sure enough, she had gotten a job. The letters were brimming with words of gratitude, saying she would remember the woman's kindness all her life. To make recompense, she insisted on leaving her bedding, clothes and personal articles for her foster grandmother. She only requested that the woman help with the procedure for transferring household registry to the city.

She listened wordlessly as the letter was read to her. That afternoon she hobbled about taking care of the household registry papers, then posted them before the evening mail pickup. She went home and laid down on the *kang* but could only feel its big emptiness. At daybreak she felt feverish all over and couldn't even rise.

She was laid up with this illness for fifteen days. When it was over she got down from the bed, white-haired and much older-looking. She had no strength to spin cotton thread. She managed to cook meals for herself, but the food had lost its savor. Xiuxiu did not write any letters after that. People in the village looked into the matter and marked the woman out for providing basic welfare benefits for the rest of her life.

She became a woman of even fewer words and went out less than before. All day long she just sat on the brick bed. The brick bed was too long — she felt it took up too much space and wasn't good for anything. The stove was also too large, and a single person did not need such a large wok. On the shelves mounted against the wall, crocks and food canisters and plates were all in a jumble. She lacked the enthusiasm and energy to straighten them up, even if she had a mind to, so she just faced them with lowered eyelids. She seemed to doze during waking hours — awake but not very clear-minded. Night and day she was in this state.

Her vision blurred but her hearing was still sharp, able

to hear the wind blow down a single leaf in the courtyard. Then she heard footsteps along the hill's edge, heading for the cave mouth. She called out, "Is that you, Wu Sanzhang?" A hand lifted the curtain in the doorway: sure enough the one who entered was Wu Sanzhang.

Wu Sanzhang was the younger brother of Wu Erzhang, with whom she had shared the "model worker" honors years ago. Erzhang had been a target of persecution during the Cultural Revolution and had died of the torments he suffered. Recently he had been vindicated posthumously, and his grave had been moved to a martyr's cemetery in the city. Thus his younger brother Sanzhang had gotten preferential treatment as a martyr's relative, so he could live comfortably. Recently he had been coming to look in on her.

"I really pity you, Big Sister. Now that Xiuxiu's mother has been vindicated and restored to her post, I don't see why you're still in such a fix. Why don't you ask them for some help?"

She just chuckled when he talked like that. "I'm getting basic benefits. What is there to ask for?"

"Where in the world is their conscience? When they have trouble, they remember you. When things go smoothly, they forget."

She had nothing to say. The two of them sat quietly for a while, then Wu Sanzhang rose to leave.

Three months later she had a relapse and could not rise from bed any longer. She knew she was not long for this world. Villagers took turns looking in on her, and Wu Sanzhang said to her: "Give Xiuxiu and her mother a call and have them send a car for you. You can try checking into a big hospital in Xi'an. Maybe you'll get better."

She did not agree and told him she had lived long enough. There was no need to tell Xiuxiu and her mother; there was still less need to get treatment in the city. Sure enough, at dawn on the third day, her vital force drained away and her breaths came haltingly. People of the village gathered around the brick bed. She said to them:

"Come up and sit on the

bed — it will hold all of you. Since you're all here to see me, I can die with my mind at ease. I only worry about Xiuxiu and her mother: if they run into trouble again after I die, whom will they turn to?"

After speaking these words, she stopped breathing. Her eyes remained open.

All of them wept. They closed her eyelids, then buried her outside the cave, at the edge of an earthen berm.

The cave was now empty, but no villagers came to live in it, so a padlock was put on the door. The years took their toll, and there was no cooking fire to keep dampness out. During a rainy spell the cave-house collapsed, burying the brick bed inside. Later, cadres from the county and province came on visits to the countryside. Quite a few female cadres who came to Yang'ergou asked about the woman. Hearing of her death and the cave's collapse, they shed tears of grief. They missed that earthen bed. They said it was a fine bed, big and comfortable.

1983

Trees Can Talk!

Jia Pingwa / 贾平凹
Translated by Nick Stember

I had come to this city to interview a commissioner, who had just retired. The interview was over, and we were sitting in his living room, drinking tea. He put on a recording and asked what I heard. I told him I heard trees in the wind. "That's right," he said. "Can you understand what the trees are saying?"

Trees give shape to the wind. But trees in the wind can talk.

You know as well as I do that this place is dirt poor. Thanks to all of the roads that pass through here, though, we have a long history of officials coming and going.

I'm already well past the age where I should be enjoying big welcomes and send-offs. When they assigned me to this post, my first thought was to take early retirement, or ask for a transfer to an unoccupied governmental position in provincial capital. You know, do some writing, spend my twilight years with my nose in a book. But after what happened the fall after I took office, though, I changed my mind. One thing led to another, and I've already been here for five years now.

What happened was this: I'd sprained my left foot while out on inspection in the countryside, and I was recuperating in my office, doing some light reading, as a matter of fact. I came across the line, "Take care of your feet, so that in youth you may bow before high officials, and serve the people until your feet are callused; and one day, ride a horse and held the reins, traveling to every corner of the land." I couldn't help but laugh out loud.

Just then someone came in to tell me an official was coming to visit from the provincial government.

It's almost a rule now that when someone important visits from the province or the capital, aside from dealing with safety precautions, you have to tidy up things around the city, clean up the streets and so on. The police chief had the peddlers and street sellers moved down to alley at the south end of the city and lined the main streets with flowers. Not having any money to renovate, meanwhile, we covered the worst parts of the city behind big posters. They also reported back that they had taken the local eccentric, a persistent petitioner, to a place 50 *li* out of the city. He was a dirty, crazy old man, and even worse, he wouldn't stop shouting about some grievance that he couldn't wait to share with the big wigs who were coming to visit.

When the official from the provincial government arrived, to our surprise, he turned out to be quite young. After getting a shot of anesthetic in my injured left foot, I submitted my progress report to our guest and with the local Party Secretary. We listened closely to his advice, writing down everything. Once we were finished, I suggested that we take him out on a tour. It was afternoon by the time we got back from visiting X County just south of the city. We were walking towards the commercial district when up ahead, at the intersection, we saw that a crowd had gathered. Someone was shouting, "Trees can talk! Trees really can talk!" I knew right away something was up, and my face turned bright red with anger. Just then, the police chief ran up and pulled me aside, letting me know that the crazy old man had found his way back to the city. He'd wrapped his arms around a telephone pole, he said, and he wouldn't let go. Everyone was out for a look. The police chief was trying to apologize, but I didn't have time to bawl him out. I hurriedly steered our visitor in the opposite direction, making a detour through another alley but we still could hear the old man shouting, "Trees can talk! Trees really can ..." followed by muffled cry, as if someone had put their hand over his mouth.

Later, while the Party Secretary introduced a row of buildings, some of which dated back to the Ming and Qing dynasties, I held back, gesturing for the police chief to come over. "Why was the crazy old man shouting that trees could talk?" I asked. He said it was all about some old tree in his village. He had been appealing to authorities about his tree for years. Everyone here knew about the old man and his tree. I asked, "How come I don't, when I've been here so long?" "A deranged old man like that? In your office?" I said, "Go tell him that he doesn't need to go looking for officials from the province and making his case out to be bigger than it is. No matter how big his grievance is, tell him to come and visit my office tonight."

That evening I dropped off our guest in his hotel to rest. Even though I was tired, I wasn't angry anymore and didn't feel much like going to sleep. Instead, I went to my office to wait for the old man. After a long time with no sign of him, I took out my brush and ink to practice my calligraphy. As commissioner, it wouldn't do for me to be seen going out dancing or playing mahjong. So after work, I had developed the habit of locking myself up in the office to read and practice calligraphy. Those are my only hobbies. I once wrote out a famous line: "On my last day, flies will serve as funeral guests; I'll die without regret only if one man knows me well." The old man arrived not long after, personally escorted by the police chief. It turned out that he had spent the afternoon locked up. I made my displeasure clear to the police chief and he apologized to the old man, who looked to be around seventy years old. He was tall and skinny, as withered as old firewood. His long hair and wild beard had grown together into a single mat, and he reeked of sweat. He didn't seem to care about being thrown in jail, and he completely ignored the police chief's apology. Instead, he shouted, "Trees can talk! The tree says it was planted in 1948!" The police chief said, "What's all that hollering? This is the commissioner!" The old man said, "Commissioner, the tree can talk!" The police chief gave him a threatening look. "This again?!" The old man thrust out his neck, the veins practically popping out. "Trees really can talk!" I said, "Fine, fine, trees can talk." The old man glared triumphantly at the police chief. He wiped at a blob of snot dangling from the tip of his nose, and made to brush it off on the table leg. Thinking better of it, he rubbed it on the seat of his pants. I invited him to sit, but he refused. The police chief said, "The commissioner wasn't asking!" Taking him by the shoulders, he pushed him into the chair. I waved my hand, gesturing for the police chief to leave before I continued my questions.

"What's your name?"

"Yang Erwa."

"What county?"

"X County, Y Township, East Hollow Village."

"How old are you?"

"Not old at all, ten days to seventy."

"What's your grievance?"

"The tree was planted in 1948, not 1952. How could it be 1952? It wasn't planted in 1952, it was planted in 1948. The tree can talk."

"Is that it?"

"That's it."

"How long have you been trying to get your case heard?"

"Fifteen years and three months."

"All that for a tree?"

"But the tree was planted in 1948, why would they say it was planted in 1952?"

"Your village should be able to handle a case like this!"

"It's all Degui's fault!"

"Who's Degui?"

"The village head. He has his eye on the tree. Wants to cut it down so he can make a coffin for his father."

"Did you talk it over with the village head?"

"They piss in the same pot!"

"Piss in the same pot?"

"Degui's wife is a whore, she and the township head ..."

"That's enough! How can you curse people like that?"

"Okay, okay. I won't curse them anymore."

"Go on then."

"I've talked to the village head thirty-two times. He finally sent his thugs to beat me up. I came to the county seat, and I talked to all the 'local magistrates' but they get transferred every two years. County Head Zhang said he'd take care of it but he got transferred. County Head Lu came next, but he said it was a matter for the village, not the county. But the village wouldn't take the case. They got me written up as a troublemaker. I'm no troublemaker. I talked to County Head Liu, County Head Wang, County Head Ma, but none of them would listen to me. They all said I was crazy. Am I crazy?"

"You're not crazy."

"I'm not! If a tree is planted in 1948, then it was planted in 1948. If I'm crazy, how come I can remember when the tree was planted?"

"The tree that you say was planted in 1948, is it still there?"

"Sure. He's getting old now though. He's got holes in him, and the branch on the east side is withered and dead. There used to be a bird nest up there, but a windstorm on that night — on the third day of the eighth lunar month — knocked it out. That should have been mine, but the village chief's son picked it up. Three days of kindling, fuck ..."

"You said the tree was planted in 1948. Do you have any proof?"

"My wife can prove it. In the spring of 1948, my wife and I went to her mom's village. I planted it after we came back. After I planted it, my wife made wide noodle stew, with chili and no salt. My wife said you just have to make do."

"How come your wife didn't come and testify?"

"She's dead. Life-long pain in the neck is what she is! Just when I need her, she goes and hangs herself! After the bitch killed herself, I couldn't be bothered to burn any paper for her. Other people's wives help out around the house and bring good luck to their husbands. But all she ever did was wait around to get fed like a pig in shit."

"Do you have any other proof?"

"The man with the dog can testify. When I was planting the tree, he was out collecting shit. But when he heard everybody else was saying the tree was planted in 1952, he claimed he couldn't remember stuff from way back when like that. Fuck the dog man! No one will back me up, but trees can talk. People just won't listen!"

"Is there anyone else in your family?"

"My son, but he's dead too. He was a good son. He was the spitting image of me, everyone in the village says so. My son came with me to the county to try my case. We took a tractor back. The tractor flipped. I was fine, but the tractor landed on my son's stomach and pushed his guts out. When my wife asked where our son was, I cursed her and she hung herself."

"Huh."

"Commissioner, I'm certain the tree was planted in 1948, not 1952. Just go and listen, trees can talk."

"Yang Erwa —"

"Uh-huh."

"Here's what we're going to do. Take this money, go to the station tomorrow and buy a ticket home. Don't go running around again. I'll send a team to find out the truth. If the tree was planted in 1948, then it was planted in 1948. If it was planted in 1952, then it was planted in 1952. Either way, we'll let you know."

"But the tree was planted in 1948! If you end up deciding the tree was planted in 1952, I'm not giving up. What's your name?"

"Hui Shiqing."

"Fine. I'll sue you all. Village Head Degui, Township Head, County Head Wang, County Head Zhang, County Head Lu, County Head Liu, County Head Ma, and you, Hui Shiqing. Commissioner Hui!"

After I'd seen off our guest from the provincial government, I called County Head Ma in X County and asked him to send me Yang Erwa's police record. County Head Ma personally came to deliver his report. He said Yang Erwa didn't have a police record, but he was familiar with his case. He said the tree was located on the south side of East Hollow village. The land it was on belonged to Yang Erwa before New China was established in 1949. The land became public property during the land reforms, but any trees on it would have remained private property. When the tree was still small nobody paid it much mind. But later, when the tree had grown up, Yang Erwa said it was planted in 1948, so it belonged to him. The other villagers said it was planted in 1952, on public land, so it should belong to the village. The long and short of it was, they had been trying to cut it down for years, but Yang Erwa always found a way to save it at the last minute. He even tore down his house and rebuilt so that the tree was now standing right in his living room.

"How much can a tree like that be worth?" County Head Ma said, "Farmers are pig-headed like that. Crazy old Yang Erwa has been trying to get his case heard for fifteen years now. Not a very meaningful life if you ask me."

"I suppose you can tell me what is?"

After chewing out my subordinates, I ordered them to put together a task force to resolve the case in East Hollow Village. "Trees have growth rings," I said. "Invite some experts to tell you whether the tree was planted in 1948 or 1952."

It wasn't long before the task force came back. They concluded that the tree was planted in 1948. In my memorandum I wrote:

The tree belongs to Yang Erwa.

And that was the end of the whole business. Or so I thought.

The next spring, X County was suffering from a serious drought, and I went out to the countryside to assess the situation. That was when I remembered Yang Erwa and the tree he planted in 1948. County Head Ma and I drove to East Hollow Village, and asked about Yang Erwa. The villagers said, "You haven't heard?"

That was when I learned that Yang Erwa had died. Skinny as he was, the old man had seemed to get around okay. But after we announced that the tree was planted in 1948 and it belonged to him, he went home, and fell ill that winter. It was a damp spring, and he only got worse. He died in bed, but nobody could say for sure when. By the time the villagers had found him he was already stiff.

County Head Ma said, "If he had kept trying his case, he might still be alive."

If that was true, then it meant I killed the old man.

I sighed. "'If a man learns the Way in the morning, he can die without regret in the evening.' Isn't that what Confucius said?" County Head Ma pointed at a dead caterpillar hanging by a thread from the tree and said, "I suppose this little bugger knows the Way then!"

If we hadn't set the record straight about the tree being planted in 1948 ... who's to say? Maybe he would have lived to one hundred, or one thousand?

The tree was still alive. It was just a common sumac, but like the old man had said, there were holes in its trunk, and the east branch was withered and dead. Now the west branch was gone, too. The bottom third of the tree disappeared into a crooked-looking shack. Since Yang Erwa didn't have any family, the villagers buried him in the floor of the shack, with an old cupboard as a coffin. They locked the door and left the shack to fall apart — a tomb of his own.

I said, "Let's pour the old man a drink."

The secretary bought me a bottle, and I emptied it out on the ground in front of his makeshift tomb. The wind picked up. You couldn't see it, but the leaves and branches of the sumac whispered and rustled, giving shape to the wind, talking in the wind. The old man had told me that trees can talk. But what would they say if they could? I couldn't make it out, so I used a tape recorder to make this recording.

I've been trying for years. Tell me, what do you think the tree is saying?

1996

Critique

A Fixed Star in the Literary Firmament

Yang Lesheng / 杨乐生
Translated by Denis Mair

In the development of contemporary literature over the past thirty years, Jia Pingwa has been a constant presence that cannot be ignored.

Over the past thirty years, Jia's performance in various creative domains has been worth taking pride in. In one-hundred-odd works running to over ten million published characters, he has moved into the foremost rank of his contemporaries and won recognition as a miracle on the Chinese literary scene. Proceeding along the multiple tracks of fiction, essays, criticism, poetry, calligraphy and ink painting, he has flowered and borne fruit in each genre. Such a phenomenon is rarely seen within the circle of Sinophone writers. People are on one hand impressed by his creativity and on the other hand are amazed at the artistic world he has constructed. Here we have a "peasant," a weak physical specimen of unremarkable physiognomy, a halting speaker, but somehow he has presented us with an ongoing literary miracle. What are we to do but exclaim at the marvel of it?! In general, for a writer to attain the apex in one genre is hard enough, but Jia Pingwa stands at the apex in many areas. Aside from concluding that he is a literary genius, we would be hard put to find a superlative that could encapsulate and assess his value. Take his essays for example. There are plenty of contemporary essayists, but if we rate them by the standard set by Jia, not many of them will measure up. The situation is similar with respect to novel-writing. These are some of the prizes Jia has won for his novels: America's Mobil Pegasus Prize (*On Edge*), France's Prix Femina (*Ruined City*), and China's Mao Dun Literature Prize (*Qin Opera*) and Dream of the Red Chamber Award (*Qin Opera*). If we make a survey of China's contemporary writers, it is not likely we will find another winner of so many top-level prizes both in China and abroad. He is one of the limited number of contemporaries whose writings are consistently translated for foreign publication. This gives us a sidelight on the breadth of Jia Pingwa's influence. It has been said that Jia is the "knight-errant" of Chinese literature. I consider this to be a trenchant assessment which is not at all effusive.

Let us speak specifically on Jia Pingwa's mastery of the short story form: he is irreplaceable due to the new artistic level to which he has taken this genre. Compilation of the present collection, first of all, faces an embarrassment of riches. Jia has written numerous short stories and novellas which have been collected in over thirty published volumes, with a word count running to three million characters. Thus one hardly knows where to begin the selection process. In the space of a limited volume, how is one to choose stories that can represent Jia's unique traits as an artist? Should one choose by period of composition? Should one focus on prize-winning pieces? Should one choose pieces that are controversial due to their spirit of aesthetic exploration? Should one focus on critical consensus or on audience reception as a basis for selection? These are concrete problems that cannot be evaded: if not handled fittingly, they will detract from the overall reading experience. The approach taken in the present collection was to solicit opinions, but only from a few advisers. No attempt was made to encompass all facets or include each creative stage; no consideration was given to subject matter; no priority was given to prize-winning pieces; and sequence of publication was not considered. Only works from his mature period were chosen, with preference given to exploratory pieces and with a secondary emphasis on typical evocations of Shangzhou and on his reality-oriented pieces. Of course, this approach is bound to omit many fine pieces and give an impression of partiality, but it is my wish that my "partiality" will hit upon a vein of high-grade artistic ore.

Jia Pingwa's most noteworthy contribution to the Chinese literary scene is his fashioning of the "world of Shangzhou" in a large number of works. If we suppose that these works are a paean to his home district, penned by its devoted son, that would be underestimating his far-reaching literary ambitions. It would also ignore his contemplative vision of modernity and his cosmopolitan outlook, which have long ago expanded beyond the geographical bounds of Shangzhou. His Shangzhou is not simply a district [containing 26 towns and townships] in northern Shaanxi province. As penned by Jia Pingwa, Shangzhou is really a window through which we can come to know China. All the transformations of Chinese society are reflected, more or less, in this body of work: it is an X-ray machine that shows us China from the inside. One could say that the pattern of events in Shangzhou is the pattern of events in China; the changes undergone by Shangzhou are those that the world undergoes. Shangzhou is the point of departure for Jia's art, but its direction goes beyond Shangzhou to cover the land mass of China and advances into the world at large. Almost all of Jia's novellas up to 1990 were about Shangzhou, and many of his short stories address the subject of Shangzhou. Classic examples of this are his masterworks — "Tiangou," "A Woman Named Black," and "Felicitous Site." These pieces in one respect are richly grounded in history; in another they embrace the here-and-now with warm regard, delving into deep-seated matters of human nature; from many angles they bring alive the people and events on this patch of land. Such personae as Tiangou, The Master's Wife, Woman-Named-Black and Liu Zhiyan carry the iconic stamp of Jia's character portrayal, which has been winning increasingly wider acknowledgement from the public. Added to this are Jia's voluminous essays and his influential novels like *On Edge*, *Old Gao Village* and *Qin Opera* which present us with a rich, multi-hued-and-layered evocation of Shangzhou. Among contemporary Chinese writers, perhaps only Mo Yan's "Gaomi Township of Dongbei" can rival Jia's imaginative construct. Taking an overview of Chinese and Western literature, we will find a shared phenomenon: Quite a few outstanding writers have created imaginary worlds of their own which are superimposed upon their home districts. For Gabriel García Márquezit it was Macondo; for William Faulkner it was Yoknapatawpha County; for Lu Xun it was Lu Town and Wei Village; for Shen Congwen it was West Hunan. These artistic worlds exceed the scope of each writer's native district *per se*, and they have found a place in readers' hearts as cultural symbols. Jia Pingwa's Shangzhou is undoubtedly an artfully created world, constituting a rich aesthetic vein with plenty of reserves yet to be unearthed. Nevertheless, we can say with assurance that as research on Jia goes deeper, the special value in his imaginative world will be brought increasingly to light.

Over several decades, Jia Pingwa has endeavored to inherit and advance the essence of China's traditional art, never ceasing for a day. He has succeeded in creating a corpus of masterworks in various genres. Whether in terms of conception or structure, of language or plotting, of description or narrative, all his works grow out of his successful exploratory integrations of the classical and the modern. Among Chinese writers he is a prime exemplar of "Chinese form" and Chinese "soul-force." In fact, we can point to him as a defining writer of our milieu. Now that the Chinese "vernacular movement" is in its one-hundredth year, those who feel concerned for Chinese literature must face a major problem: has the modern Sinitic language made adequate strides in its development? If a solution is not found to this problem, then all talk of Chinese literature's modernization is baseless. Everyone knows that literature is the art of language, but as for how to reach an artistic plane in language, to speak is much easier than to act. We need only look at how many or few writers in the 20th century have forged their own linguistic personality to realize the gravity and urgency of this problem. It is regrettable that in the case of most writers, even well-known ones, we can hardly speak of literary personality, let alone the distinctiveness that enables us to identify an unattributed piece of writing. From the "May Fourth New Culture Movement" in 1919 right up to the present day, there have only been ten-or-so figures whose writing makes our eyes light up in recognition, namely Hu Shi, the Zhou brothers (Zhou Zuoren and Zhou Shuren), Lao She, Shen Congwen, Wang Zengqi, Jin Yong, Wang Xiaobo, Jia Pingwa and a few others. I hope my view on this does not prove to be one-sided and prejudiced.

Our modern and contemporary fiction writers and essayists have been pervasively influenced by "Europeanization" and

Soviet-era literature. Their language, for the most part, can be called a Sinitic version of European and American language. This is sometimes called "translationese" : it is a far cry from the inherent features of the Chinese language, and it has not inherited its soul-force in a satisfactory way. This is not to say that writing in old-style Chinese cannot exist in a contemporary context. What I am emphasizing here is the utilization and development of modern Sinitic in literary writing. I am convinced that language determines the height to which literature can develop. This is not an issue of standardization; it is a matter of poetic and aesthetic substance. As a people the Chinese have generated forms touching on many areas, and literary language is only one such form, albeit an important one. I do not presume to say that Jia's attempts at a "vernacular-classical hybrid" mode are uniformly successful, but no one can deny his exploratory spirit and consistently industrious efforts. Anyone with eyes to see will appreciate other aspects of his talent, such as the techniques of rough sketching in his writing. Another appealing feature of his fiction is the way he draws on and goes beyond the mythic-and-grotesque stories in the Northern and Southern Dynasties, romances of the Tang-and-Song era and literary sketches in the Ming-and-Qing era. *Record of Taibai* is a series of twenty short stories: they are penned in an accomplished yet casual manner, short but incisive, giving one the sense of a new style of the "mythic-and-grotesque" . There is an empathy toward the realities of existence, but at the same time there are Buddhist ideas, imbued with a zen-like sense of intuitive enlightenment. Amid the mélange of oddities, one also finds cogitation in a rationally modern vein. Amid critical trains of thought one can sense the writer's tolerance and tenderness. After going through these pieces, the reader feels refreshed and energized. Some may hold the opinion that Jia Pingwa likes to traffic in the supernatural and deliberately plays with a mystical bag of tricks. Aren't they aware that starting from *Classic of Mountains and Seas* and *In Search of the Marvelous*, unbridled imaginings and fantasy elements have long been a feature of Chinese fiction? Mysticism is an inalienable component of Chinese culture, for there are many things in life which are inherently hard to explain. We could plausibly say that in such subject matter, Jia has found a path of development for modern Chinese fiction. As for how to press forward on this path, only time will tell.

While exerting his full energy to pursue literary "Chineseness," Jia Pingwa never forgets to infuse his short fiction with modern awareness that supports it from within. At first glance, it would seem that Jia's writings all deal with rural villages and peasants. There is nothing strange about this, because China has eight-to-nine hundred million peasants, which means that 40% of the world's total number of farmers live in China. For a contemporary writer to concern himself with farmers is a rightful obligation and a heaven-given vocation. Like Shen Congwen, who called himself a "man of the countryside," Jia Pingwa once declared, "I am a peasant." These four words happen to be the title of one of his books. Such a moniker does not just represent his fondness for rural people, it is also a sign of his humility, his homespun traits and his unassuming outlook. The crux of rural subject matter does not lie in whether you write about peasants but how you write about them, and what artistic conceptions you employ in writing about them. Way back around 1980, Jia had already made up his mind to update his literary conceptions, and out of this came stories like "Sandy Ground," "Elegy for Old Lady Xia Wu," "February Almonds," and "The Won-Done Song." These stirred up controversy and moved toward the cutting edge of fiction at the time. In his fictional creation he was obviously influenced by Japan's Yasunari Kawabata and the Latin American writers Vargas Llosa and Juan Rulfo, especially Kawabata's artistic ideal and pursuit of "Japanization." His serial stories on Shangzhou such as "A Woman Named Black" and "Tiangou" are representative of the modern mentality of his writing. The abundance and complexity of character types, with the concurrent delving into human nature are salient features of his writings from that period. As for his short fiction after 1990, it can no longer be subsumed under "naturalism" or any other simple term. Far from being monochrome, it is many-hued, many-sided and richly varied. It is a new entity compounded of China's cultural spirit blended with modernity. Jia Pingwa applied himself to absorbing and even "appropriating" modern artistic concepts, forms and techniques from other lands. Although such combinations may come off somewhat stiffly in certain pieces such as "Evening Song" and "Sufferer" , they fully embody his personality, which is cautious in matters of everyday life yet bold and surprisingly innovative in his artistic creations. "Tobacco" is not an ordinary psychological story, and it cannot be summed up as "stream of consciousness." What I value is the way he utilizes the Buddhist idea of reincarnation in the story. More than that, I like the dreamlike, swirling succession of life encounters. As for "A Story Someone Told Me," one of his recent efforts, it is a short, exquisite piece in which three story arcs are braided together. It is ageless yet modern, combining the native and the cosmopolitan. Its broad vision points directly at the predicament of human existence and the absurd inanities people get mired in. It is tender-hearted yet aggrieved; the writing shows practiced ease; the narrative is spare. This is clearly a work that was long-incubated yet spontaneously released: it could only have been written by a consummate craftsman. A concern for all things human has long been the overarching theme of fiction. The modern conception of the human has advanced from that of tradition, so the range of concerns is richer. To delve into all that is human is Jia's constant endeavor. From his early character Wang Mantang to a recent one like Han Qixiang, he works on many levels, making us recognize and appreciate the boundless reaches of the human spiritual world. The multifarious human types in China, especially those of society's lower stratum, have always been his key objects of observation and concern as a writer. Over decades he has groped and trudged and tumbled along the rough, roundabout path that has brought him to the present. He has reached the level at which his fiction can purify and cleanse mental state and emotion without contrivance, in an unprecedented way that merges naturalism, mysticism, realism and modernism. In contemporary Chinese literature, he looms as a mountain that no one can skirt without climbing.

We should examine Jia Pingwa the Writer together with Jia Pingwa the Artist. This article merely presents a rough discussion of his short fiction, so it cannot present a vision of the whole picture. In a cultural sense, the Jia who constructs the fictional world of Shangzhou and the one who transcends it are connected but not equivalent. Due to their artistic merit, a large number of his short stories and novellas have been adapted into movies and TV series, stage plays and dance dramas, thereby broadening their influence on society. Right now it is hard to predict what surprises this outstandingly talented and hard-working writer has in store for us. At any rate, there is still plenty of space in which literary studies on Jia's oeuvre can unfold: to say there are unbounded prospects for research would be no exaggeration. In the past the term "fixed star" gave one the impression of an unmoving celestial body, and only planets were thought of as moving. By now scientists have observed that fixed stars are not just emitters of light and heat: they too move through space at various speeds. It is my heartfelt wish that Jia Pingwa will be recognized as a fixed star sending out beams in all directions.

Interview

An Interview with Jia Pingwa

Shu Jinyu / 舒晋瑜

Translated by Ella Schwalb

Shu Jinyu: With the publication of your 16th novel, the lengthy *Shan Ben*, many people's first reaction has been: Master Jia is incredibly industrious. Seeing the densely packed characters of your manuscript — especially given the fact that it is handwritten — one can't help but admire your perseverance, the depth of your devotion to writing. If you had to describe it, what is it that really attracts you to writing? Is it a kind of bliss of expression, the relief of finding a spiritual abode in written language?

Shu Jinyu / 舒晋瑜

Jia Pingwa: The writing process is a moment of communion with the soul. Other people are seeing arduous work, but actually my body and mind have this kind of unspeakable joy. Having written for a few decades, it's already become a habit for me, a way of life. As far as how I can write so much? You must approach life with a perceptive mind and a sensitive heart; to devote yourself to writing you must foster a feeling of hunger.

Shu Jinyu: When I read your book *Shan Ben*, the strongest feeling was this very profound life in there, like a dense mountainous forest enshrouded in mist. Within the detailed writing, one finds the mishaps of social relations, the ways of the world, the nature of its people and the reasons for human life, whether obvious or hidden. The relationships between man and nature, the world, fellow man, and the times are all interrelated, tangled up in one another. In your writing process, does the state of your heart tend to be more ambiguous, or more clear and discerning?

Jia Pingwa: In the end, it's all about writing yourself. The depth and magnitude of your work is dictated by your energy, your field of vision, your understanding of nature and of life. As someone who has been writing for a few decades, and at this stage of my life, there are some things I will just see right through — I have my experience and insight. However, there are even more things that still leave me puzzled; I am trying to get closer to them, to understand them. I yearn for them.

Shu Jinyu: Your novels are very long, but within them all, I can see traces of prose and of poetry. I am among the many readers who are also passionate enthusiasts of your essays, which are unique, having the beauty of a plain, light simplicity. How do you see the distinctions and connections between the genres of essay, fiction, and poetry? In your own personal writing, how do you reconcile the three?

Jia Pingwa: I don't want to make such clear-cut distinctions between genres in my writing. The purview of any piece of writing is the same; they differ in nothing more than length and structure. It's not that I reconcile them on purpose; I'm just following my heart, writing offhand.

Shu Jinyu: The fine points of classical literature can be read in your writing style. So

I can't help but wonder: you must have studied the original canon of various pre-Qin sages, *The Book of Songs*, etc. You practice calligraphy, you collect antiques — I suppose you're really nurturing a certain air about you. This air surely transfers, infusing your writing. Could I see it that way? Would you say that the wellspring of your literary world is folklife, natural landscapes, classic characters, and divine craftsmanship?

Jia Pingwa: You could see it that way. Writing, calligraphy, painting, collecting, etc., these are all born out of interest, out of my natural disposition. In fact that's how all aesthetic taste is. I believe when working on any form of art there must necessarily be an interplay between the modern, the traditional, and the folk.

Shu Jinyu: Reading your fiction of the past few years, one gets the sense that you are gradually starting to ponder more and more the contrast between nature and human affairs, that there is more intimacy with and reverence for mountains and rivers. For example your line: "The mountain ridge spans the place eternally like a dragon, guiding the Yangtze and Yellow Rivers, commanding the North and the South. This is the Qinling mountain range, China's grandest mountains." What is your own feeling about this transformation of yours?

Jia Pingwa: When you first learn to write, you think you already know it all, that you're omnipotent. But the more you write, the more you realize your own ignorance and insignificance. The more you write the more you have this kind of awe, the awe of the natural world, the awe of society, the awe of writing. Work is often accomplished in this kind of awe. You may just be trying to express your own experiences and realizations, rather than writing a romance or a few beautiful sentences to please readers.

Shu Jinyu: In recent years, many have bemoaned the demise of really powerful Shaanxi writers like Mr. Chen Zhongshi (陈忠实) and Mr. Hong Ke (红柯), calling to mind the frailty and ephemerality of life. As a friend, colleague, and, on some level, also as one another's literary soul mates, there's no way you've remained unmoved. When it comes to matters of life and death, what kind of view do you take, be it from a philosophical or pragmatic perspective?

Jia Pingwa: Every person will die, it's very ordinary. But when a close friend dies, it still shocks and grieves us; a part of us dies with them. As one poet said: Life is like a splendid summer blossom, death is like a beautiful, motionless autumn leaf. While alive, one must live to the fullest. Facing death, one must be tranquil and serene. This is the most perfect existence.

Shu Jinyu: A writer must work within history and seek wisdom from the past, while at the same time live in the current reality, as it's very difficult to remain unaffected by the present era. You "created" the writer Jia Pingwa, and in turn the writer Jia Pingwa has become you — the one cannot be separated from the other. As far as being a person living in our present reality, has literature helped you in any way to better get along with the times, serving as a major buffer?

Jia Pingwa: Authors get along with the times through literature, sorting out their judgment on the era through their work while also sorting out themselves. As they record the times through their work, they are also recording themselves. When writing attempts to influence the pilgrimage towards our ideals, this brings with it the writer's own pilgrimage. When you expel the poison from your own soul in a piece of writing, you are simultaneously driving off the poisons of our society.

Shu Jinyu: In *Shan Ben*, you're writing a biography of the Qin Mountain in the form of fiction, and Bashu is also intimately tied to these mountains. These past few years, you have frequently gone to Sichuan, to Bashu. What kind of magnetic pull do you see Bashu as having on your spirit?

Jia Pingwa: Bashu is both grand and mystical. There is a glorious history, there are many literary giants who have come out of Bashu, and there is the beauty of its landscapes. I yearn for it all. I've gone on more than 10 trips traveling to many different places there, and I still want to go back for more. Traveling along famous rivers, discussing wonderful books, meeting the greats: these are all good nourishments for cultivating my noble spirit!

Shu Jinyu: Your daughter Jia Qianqian also writes poetry and has been well-received by the professional poetry circle. How do you feel as a father, observing your daughter's literary talent from the sidelines?

Jia Pingwa: As far as my daughter's talent being on display, I am both gratified and anxious because there's a lot of pressure as well as a lot of squabbling when you get into literary circles. I wish just for her happiness, comfort, and peace.

Culture & Heritage

An Incredible Marvel of the East

Li Denan / 李德楠
Translated by Fernando Arrieta

The waters of the great canal irrigate the whole region. On some of its sections the canal is so wide and the water so plentiful that it is impossible to see the far bank. And even where it is possible to glimpse it, it is barely discernible. All those wide sections are navigable, and there is always a large number of ships on the canal: it is an incredible sight. What I mean to say is that, in this respect, the canal is like no other in the world. I once stayed for eight days by the canal's lower reaches, between Nanjing and Hangzhou. As I waited there, I saw an astonishing number of ships sailing on the canal. In the time it took an hourglass to empty, I could count more than three hundred ships, and those were only the ones sailing upstream. The ships were all

Li Denan / 李德楠

packed with either goods or travelers. It was a true wonder to see.

This is how Álvaro Semedo (1585–1658) — Portuguese priest, Jesuit missionary, and author of *The History of that Great and Renowned Monarchy of China* — described the Grand Canal. Between 1616 and 1620, he went to China twice to carry out his missionary work, visiting Hangzhou, Jiading, Shanghai, Nanjing, and their surroundings.

The Chinese say that in the past, the area was a vast expanse of water. With the use of large amounts of labor, much of that water was pushed back into the sea, and what was left was forced to flow through the many canals that have been opened everywhere. It was all accomplished by the local population with very little training in the principles of physics and hydraulics. That they have accomplished such a mighty feat of engineering is indeed incredible. The canals are, for the most part, straight and neatly arranged. To drain off flood water and protect the canals, people have built other waterways to connect them to rivers. There is no doubt that the local people's ingenuity and resourcefulness have contributed to those achievements.

So wrote the French Jesuit missionary Louis Le Comte (1655–1728). He came to China in 1685 to serve as a mathematician in the court of Emperor Kangxi, returning to France in 1692.

[The] Grand Canal, an inland navigation of such extent and magnitude as to stand unrivalled in the history of the world ... I may safely say that, in point of magnitude, our most extensive inland navigation of England can no more be compared to the grand trunk that intersects China, than a park or garden pond to the great lake of Windermere ... [T]he conception of such an undertaking, and the manner in which it is executed, imply a degree of science and ingenuity beyond what I suspect we should now find in the country, either in one or the other of these people.

These words were written in 1804 by the British diplomat and writer Sir John Barrow

(1764–1848). In 1793, Barrow traveled to China as a member of Lord George Macartney's first British diplomatic mission to the country, serving as comptroller of Macartney's household. He voyaged south along the Grand Canal, from Beijing to Hangzhou.

When describing China's Grand Canal, these 17th-century European missionaries and 18th-century British diplomat all expressed great amazement at this mighty engineering project of the East. Thanks to an abundance of manpower, the scale of China's ancient public works was gigantic; other countries' engineering projects seemed to pale in comparison. For instance, 2,000 years ago, China had already built a huge defensive wall, known as the Great Wall, which stretched for thousands of miles. Four centuries before the first canals were built in Europe, China had already opened a vast number, connecting rivers within the country, providing irrigation for crops, draining off floodwater, and serving as transportation routes. The people who accomplished these engineering feats had received no formal education in the principles of physics or engineering, and often proceeded based on their own instincts and experience. As they worked on their construction, they found solutions not even the most ingenious theories could provide.

China was one of the first civilizations to build canals, alongside ancient Egypt and Babylon. The Han Conduit (Han Gou), built in 486 BCE, was the first section of what was to become the Grand Canal, and today it is still an important waterway connecting the provinces of Jiangsu and Anhui. In 610 CE, after several centuries of expansion and maintenance work, the rulers of the Sui Dynasty completed a canal that, with the capital Luoyang as its central hub, stretched to Beijing in the north and Hangzhou in the south, with a total length of 2,700 kilometers. This was the first Grand Canal. In 1293, Kublai Khan, emperor of the Yuan Dynasty, shortened the distance between Beijing and Hangzhou to 1,794 kilometers

Hangzhou Terminal of the Grand Canal (站酷海洛)

by opening new sections that ran through Tianjin, Hebei, Shandong, Jiangsu, Zhejiang, and other cities and provinces, and crossed five large river systems — those of the Hai, the Yellow, the Huai, the Yangtze, and the Qiantang.

The rulers of the two dynasties that followed the Yuan, the Ming and the Qing, spared no effort in maintaining the canal and keeping the waterways open. Today, a section north of the city of Jining is no longer navigable due to low water levels; but the section south of Jining and down to Hangzhou has been upgraded with large-capacity water locks and major water conservancy infrastructure, and is currently open to traffic.

During the 16th and 17th centuries, England and other European countries, such as France, Germany, Italy, and the Netherlands, underwent rapid industrialization. In order to meet the transportation needs created by increased trade, they built a large number of canals. But none was a match for China's Grand Canal in terms of length, antiquity, and the sheer scale of the engineering works required for its construction.

By the 18th century, the Grand Canal had become a vital link between northern and southern China. The opening of new sections had connected all of China's major waterways and created a true transportation network crossing China's two major rivers, the Yangtze and the Yellow River, taking a steady flow of grain and other products of the south to the capital in the north, while also promoting migration and the economic development of many port cities along its banks. The construction of those new canal sections overcame many natural obstacles, turning rivers and lakes into navigable links and incorporating them into the Grand Canal itself. Their construction was a wonder in the history of engineering, and bear witness to the industriousness, willpower, and resourcefulness of the Chinese people.

On June 22, 2014, during the thirty-eighth session of the UNESCO World Heritage Committee, the Grand Canal became the forty-sixth Chinese monument to be added to the World Heritage List. The Grand Canal as a listed monument includes twenty-seven sections of the canal itself, traversing twenty-seven cities and eight different provinces, as well as many examples of water conservancy infrastructure and other auxiliary buildings, adding up to a total of fifty-eight specific sites and a total canal length of 1,011 kilometers.

Compared with the canals of other countries, China's Grand Canal follows a much more meandering route, and because it also follows the course of several rivers, it is also much less uniform in breadth. These, however, are not its only particularities. China's Grand Canal has a much longer history, having been built over 2,000 years ago; the strict system of traffic management under which it operated over the centuries was unique. The profound economic and political influence it has had on China also marks it apart from other historical canals. Today, more than 300 million Chinese still live in the regions that border the Grand Canal. The Canal is itself a record of the history and life of these people, and it is also a source of knowledge that explains many of China's mysteries. Its origins can be traced back to the 5th century BCE, and since then it has witnessed countless moments of historical significance in the history of China, moments that have determined its tortuous course.

Life along the Grand Canal

Li Denan / 李德楠
Translated by Jun Liu / 刘　浚

The Grand Canal runs for well over a thousand kilometers across the vast landmass of China. Adorning the canal are cities like pearls on a string, a kaleidoscope of cargo, and flocks of people from all walks of life. This is not a static structure — the Grand Canal is full of human vitality. There are people who work the canal, who live upon it, and who travel for leisure along it. Together they form a lively "Tableau of Life along the Grand Canal."

1. Laborers

The Grand Canal is a man-made river whose massive engineering scale and great length required a huge amount of labor from the very beginning of its construction. Once completed, more hands were needed for its function and maintenance. It was these ordinary Chinese — nameless in historical accounts — who made the world-renowned Grand Canal a reality.

Drawing upon the country's vast labor pool, and driven by his own ambition and determination, Emperor Yang of the Sui Dynasty was able to complete the canal's northern and southern sections in just six years (AD 605–610). According to *The*

Annals of Emperor Yang (*Book of Sui*, Vol Ⅲ), in March of the First Year of the Daye Era, over one million men and women from various prefectures of Henan were mobilized to build the Tongji Channel; more than one hundred thousand Huainan residents were then assembled to construct the Han Conduit. In the Fourth Year of the Daye Era, an imperial decree conscripted another one million laborers from prefectures in Hebei to dig the Yongji Channel. Later on in the Yuan Dynasty, the full span of the Grand Canal — known as the Jinghang Canal since it connected Beijing and Hangzhou — was completed and entered operation, and it was thoroughly dredged during the Ming Dynasty. Such colossal projects would have been unthinkable without millions of laborers. Like the legend of Mengjiangnü whose tears were said to have crumbled the Great Wall when she learned of her husband's demise during its construction, the Grand Canal also engendered numerous heartrending tales. This was especially so during the Sui Dynasty when projects became so demanding that no less than a million persons are believed to have perished.

Massive amounts of drafted labor were called for, and not just to build the canal. Its maintenance and subsequent dredging also involved big numbers of workers. The Ming Government kept up to 50,000 people in mandatory service, assigning them tasks such as building and repairing embankments; opening and shutting sluice gates; pulling boats across the weirs; and keeping the water source clean. In addition, a sizeable population of dockhands, sailors, boat trackers, porters, boatmen and other menial workers was scattered along the Grand Canal.

Life on the canal was basic and impoverished. The boatmen and trackers who worked and lived for years along its meandering banks composed their own "Grand Canal Chants." When the season came to transport grain northward to the capital, tens of thousands of barges would gather amid outbursts of song by the coolies that echoed in the port cities, constituting a unique auditory and visual tableau on the Grand Canal.

In Chinese, the word "*hao*" (号) means to yell, to call on everyone to join hands to accomplish a single task. With a suffix the word becomes "*haozi*," (号子) the sound of calling or shouting. On the canal, such "*haozi*" were essentially work songs that served to command and coordinate those who rowed or pulled the boats. There were chants for almost every occasion: "Setting Sail Chant" could be heard as a boat readied to leave port; "Oar-Rowing Chant" might be needed as the boat flowed down a slow section of a river; "Rope-Pulling Chant" was for trackers pulling a boat against the current; and if a craft became stranded, a "Boat-Pushing Chant" was sure to be heard. When it came to unloading, other chants accompanied the act of transporting cargo out of the hull, loading the burden onto the shoulder, and carrying grain across the ever-shifting gangplank.

The Canal Chants were typically improvised with a free-flowing tune, their tempo and speed depending on the nature of the task. One man initiated the song, and his fellow workers soon joined in chorus. Simple lyrics with catchy rhymes were employed, and the tune was highly charged with rhythm and gusto. The following "Oar-Rowing Chant" is a good example:

Yo ha-ha, hoh!

Grip the oar 'n' let it fly, bend over double 'n' set the feet wide;

Don't scramble to row forw'd, extend the arms 'n' push it right!

Yo — yo — hoh!

The simple lyrics above serve as a rhythmic reminder to the oarsmen to paddle in concert with one another. The following *Canal Trackers' Ballad*, however, does more than just function to synchronize the trackers. It recounts highlights of their earlier voyage and seeks to inspire enthusiasm via the tale of how King Wen of Zhou convinced Grand Duke Jiang to join him in overthrowing the Shang Dynasty.

Hi-ya-ha-hi!

Stoop the shoulders 'n' bend o' er double,

Steady each foot 'n' clutch the rope.

Hi-ya-ha-hi!

Pulling the boat one stop aft another, the cutting wind not a bother.

Loading dates in Linqing, we sailed down south to Hangzhou;

Loading rice in Hangzhou, we pulled it north to Beijing.

Aye-ya-ha-hi.

Dragon-like the Grand Canal runs for a thousand miles.

Clutch the rope 'n' ne'er let go,

Like King Wen dragging the Grand Duke.

The King dragged the Duke for eight hundred steps,

The Duke secured the kingdom for eight hundred years.

Aye-ya-ha-hi!

From the mid-19th century onward, sediment accumulated in the Grand Canal and the transport of imperial grain gradually ground to a halt. This was a severe blow to the livelihood of tens of thousands of sailors, boatmen and trackers along the waterway. Many of them gravitated to secret societies such as the "Cao Gang" in the Qing Dynasty, forerunner of the Republican Era's "Green Gang."

2. Boat People

Among the groups of people who relied upon the Grand Canal's network, the boatmen, sailors and the Cao Gang were important forces to reckon with due to their huge numbers. There were also the so-called "boat people" who eked out a living with their vessels, either transporting cargo, or catching and raising fish. Most lacked the economic means to settle on land, so they called their boats their home and spent their lives drifting on water.

Jiangsu and Zhejiang along the eastern coast were endowed with an intricate cobweb of waterways, and the Grand Canal strengthened connections between those rivers and lakes.

The resulting network attracted large numbers of boat people like a magnet. Life aboard a vessel was one of hardship. In the old days, there was a saying in China: "There are three bitter ways of earning a living — punting a boat, hammering iron, and grinding beans to make tofu." Topping the list was propelling a boat with a long pole. The boat people followed a set of folk customs, shaped by their ever-changing habitat on water, which distinguished them from land-dwellers.

Most boat people rose at sunrise and called an end to their workday at sunset. Living on the water day in, day out, they sometimes referred to their vessel as *lian jia chuan* (连家船) — boat-cum-home. They fished on their floating home, cooked and slept there, together with their dogs and cats; some even housed pigs, ducks and geese. Normally, the bow was for fishing, the covered midsection served as sleeping quarters, and the stern was for cooking. On the Grand Canal, it was common to see a husband or wife standing at the bow to propel the boat, while the other rowed the scull at the stern, singing in perfect synchronization.

When the children of a boat family grew up, most would marry within the boat-dwelling community. On the wedding day, the two ships would moor on opposite banks. Then the bride, adorned with an elaborate "phoenix coronet" and donning a bright red padded jacket, would be ferried to her financé's family boat. In the cabin of the groom's boat, the couple kowtowed to Heaven, Earth, the Boat Buddha and each other, and then it was time for the feast with endless toasts and abundant blessings. When the two boats parted ways the following day, the bride was hence a member of her husband's family.

While fishing nets were widely employed, the boat people also trained an aquatic bird — the cormorant — to do the heavy lifting. Below the chin of the cormorant is a roomy throat sac where the bird temporarily stores its catch. The fisherman would carefully place a ring around the bird's neck, so that the cormorant could not

Fisherman and the Cormorants (高品图像)

swallow its kill, allowing its master to retrieve the uneaten fish. When the hunt was over, the master would remove the ring, and reward the faithful but frustrated bird with fingerlings.

Life on water entailed many dangers absent on land. A boat song describes the perils:

A fishing boat tiny 'n' small,
Day 'n' night sailing off shore.
Rain-soaked meals for a hungry belly,
No inch of deck dry for a head sleepy.
This wretched life seems a blessing
When gales send waves a crashing.

It was in such a vulnerable environment that profound aversion of taboos took hold of the boat people, who venerated a special idol.

The boat people worshiped the Boat Buddha, or the boat's "Master." This deity was enshrined in the central cabin, where incense burned year-round to safeguard the boat. When a new vessel was transferred from dry dock to water, it must be launched on an auspicious day ordained by the lunar calendar. A grand ceremony was held on the occasion to offer tributes to the "Four Golden Dragon Kings" who ruled the water world. A giant "*xi*" character, standing for happiness, was pasted on the cabin door draped with a red satin ribbon. Besides the incense and red candles, offerings also included the Three Sacrificial Animals — pig head, chicken and carp. Amid thundering firecrackers, the Boat Buddha was ushered on board.

The boat people observed numerous taboos: When eating a fish, never turn it over, or you risked flipping the boat itself; similarly, upsetting a bowl was a premonition of an upturned boat; and leaving the chopsticks horizontally on a bowl was not good manners to say the least. On any fishing boat, iron chains were seldom seen while ropes were ubiquitous. This was because folklore portrayed ghosts of hell ensnaring a living man's soul with iron chains, hence ropes were deemed more auspicious. When a bridge was sighted, there were several associated superstitions and rules. If a dog was spotted running quickly across the bridge, this signaled a good day of business; but if the canine was sighted looking hesitantly in all directions, a day's hard work might net few profits. If a peasant happened to carry two night soil buckets on a shoulder pole across the bridge, but the containers were swinging back and forth, that was bad luck — the empty load signified no fish would be caught that day. And when passing by a bridge under construction, no one on board should utter a word.

Today, there are still many people living aboard their boats along the Grand Canal. Whether fishing or transporting cargo, they still spend the better part of their lives on deck. Compared to their forefathers, today's boat people might be less constrained by taboos and customs, but a tight bond still connects them to the ancient canal.

3. Visitors from afar

When the full length of the Grand Canal opened to navigation in AD 610, it immediately became China's most important artery. During the Sui and Tang dynasties, China's nobility, high-ranking officials, prominent merchants and commoners were not alone in traversing the man-made waterway. Visiting monarchs, envoys and groups of traders from Silla (Korea), Japan, the Arab Empire, Persia, Hinduk (India) and other nations were frequent passengers as well.

During the Yuan Dynasty, the Grand Canal was shortened into a straighter route and became known as the Jinghang Grand Canal. Renovations during the Ming Dynasty thoroughly dredged and unclogged the waterway, transforming it into the country's most efficient and convenient highway, unrivaled on land or water. Merchants dealing in salt and other goods, members of the literati and contenders for the Imperial Examination all left their traces alongside those of common travelers. Even the Emperor would occasionally cruise on the canal with an entourage of royalty and senior officials. Then of course, adventurers, missionaries, trade groups and diplomatic missions from foreign lands also regularly sailed the channel.

Among overseas visitors were the 13th-century Italian explorer Marco Polo and Britain's 18th-century Macartney Mission, and a host of others. What brought them to China, and for what tales did the Grand Canal serve as a backdrop?

Odorico da Pordenone (1265–1331), a Franciscan friar born in what is today's Italy, was commissioned by Pope Nicholas IV to journey eastward and chronicle religious activities. Around 1318, he set out from Venice, crossed Eurasia and eventually reached Guangzhou in southeast China. From there he traveled overland along the coast northward, stopping at Quanzhou, Fuzhou and Hangzhou before taking the Grand Canal towards Dadu (modern-day Beijing), the Yuan capital. The cruise along the canal went smoothly. Along the way, he visited several important cities including Zhejiang's Hangzhou, Jiangsu's Yangzhou, and Jining and Linqing in Shandong. While gathering information on religious life, he also noted local culture and conditions. The friar stayed at a Catholic church in the capital for three years before going back to Italy in about 1330.

Back home, Odorico dictated accounts of his journey to the East, leaving behind various manuscripts and printed versions that were widely circulated in Europe. Those relating to China would go on to inspire *The Travels of Sir John Mandeville*, a classic travelogue of medieval Europe and a testimony to early Western impressions of China.

Matteo Ricci (1552–1610), a Jesuit missionary also from Italy, was dispatched to China in 1583, where he stayed until he died of illness. Known in China as Li Madou (利玛窦), his mission was to introduce Christian teachings to the Middle Kingdom, and he established Catholic outposts in cities such as Zhaoqing, Shaozhou, Nanchang and Nanjing. Keen to promote the missionary cause, he decided to head north and seek an audience with the ruling Emperor Wanli of Ming in order to gain official recognition for Catholicism. In 1598 and 1600, he sailed the Grand Canal twice. On the second voyage, he gained an audience with Emperor Wanli and realized his aim. After Ricci, many more missionaries arrived in China to spread the Gospel. Because of the convenient transportation, the regions along the Grand Canal became the heartland of Christianity in China.

Matteo Ricci (FOTOE)

His two voyages on the Jinghang Grand Canal offered Ricci ample chance to make keen observations and stimulate profound thinking. He recognized that this waterway was constructed primarily to transport cargo from the empire's southern reaches to the capital in the north. The tens of thousands of ships plying the channel weren't just transporting tribute rice and grains to the nation's sovereign, however; a large number were commercial vessels that belonged to personages occupying various rungs on the ladder of officialdom, as well as private owners. Under constant threat from both the Yellow River and man-made traffic jams, ensuring the viability of transport on the Grand Canal generated staggeringly high costs. Ricci was perplexed by one question: Why not choose an ocean route to Beijing that would be shorter and more economical? The answer to this famous "Ricci's Puzzle," according to the man himself, was a deep-rooted "Thalassophobia" — intense fear of the sea — among the Chinese, who also loathed pirates. This question would later inspire many academic debates about inland waterways vs. oceanic transport.

Besides missionaries, foreign passengers on the canal included envoys and groups of merchants from neighboring tributary states. Prior to the end of the 19th century, East Asia maintained an international order in which China was the center of a tributary system. This evolved into a form of bilateral tributary trade. From the Ming Dynasty onwards, each tributary state would dispatch a mission every few years to present tributes to Beijing as a way of acknowledging China's dominant position. In return, the Chinese government would reciprocate with more precious wares, in keeping with the principle of "giving more and receiving less." Such states included Luzon, Sulu, Champa, Siam, Java and Sumatra in Southeast Asia, as well as Korea, Japan and Ryukyu in East Asia.

Arriving via the Grand Canal, these tributary missions entered the capital and then left on it as well, proceeding southward and trading in port cities along the way. Leaving behind an assortment of rare jewels and special produce from faraway lands, they took home Chinese products such as silk and porcelain from all across the ancient empire. The Jinghang Grand Canal thus became a vital channel for interaction between China and the rest of the world.

An Introduction to Confucius and His *Analects*

Burton Watson

Introduction

Lunyu, or *The Analects of Confucius*, has probably exercised a greater influence on the history and culture of the Chinese people than any other work in the Chinese language. Not only has it shaped the thought and customs of China over many centuries, but it has played a key role in the development of other countries that were within the Chinese cultural sphere, such as Korea, Japan, and, later, Vietnam.

Readers encountering the text for the first time might wonder how this rather brief collection of aphorisms and historical anecdotes could have been so influential. The text, probably compiled in stages some time during the fourth century B.C.E., was at first only one of many philosophical works that embodied the teachings of this or that school of early Chinese thought. The followers of the teachings of Confucius were referred to collectively as the *Ru* (儒) school, which denotes persons who devote themselves to learning and the peaceful arts (as opposed to martial matters).

Some centuries later, when Emperor Wu (r. 141–87 B.C.E.) of the Han dynasty declared Confucianism the official doctrine of the state, the *Analects* and other texts associated with Confucius assumed enormous importance. They were regarded as repositories of knowledge of how the empire had been governed in the model eras of antiquity and how the Chinese government system, and society as a whole, should be ordered. In still later centuries, the *Analects* was treated as a beginning text in the study of classical Chinese, to be committed to memory and, when students were more advanced, studied exhaustively and with its lessons examined in depth.

Confucius

According to tradition, Confucius was born in 551 B.C.E. His family name was Kong; his personal name, Qiu; and his polite name (the name by which most persons would have addressed him), Zhongni. The name Confucius is a Latinized form of Kong fuzi, or Respected Master Kong, a title commonly used to refer to him in Chinese.

Confucius was born in the small feudal state of Lu, situated in northeastern China in the area of present-day Shandong Province. His father, who was a member of the *shi* (士) class, the lowest rank of the nobility, died when Confucius was very young. It is clear from the *Analects* that Confucius grew up in considerable poverty, an experience that seems to have made him particularly sensitive to matters of wealth and class. At an early age, as he tells us, he devoted himself to learning, and the importance of education is a major theme in the *Analects*.

The extent to which this "learning" related to written texts and to which it was based on oral traditions is unclear. The *Analects* refers frequently to two texts, the *Book of Odes* (诗经) and the *Book of Documents* (书经), both of which Confucius, according to legend, had some hand in editing. A third early text, the *Book of Changes* (易经), is mentioned in one version of the *Analects*. These constitute three of what later became known as the five Confucian Classics, the other two being the *Spring and Autumn Annals* (春秋), a chronicle of the state of Lu said to have been edited by Confucius, and the *Book of Rites* (礼记), a collection of texts on ritual.

Whether Confucius's learning derived from written texts or from oral traditions, he appears to have been intensely concerned with those that reflected the early culture of China, particularly that of the sage rulers Yao and Shun of high antiquity and of the early rulers of the Xia, Yin, and Zhou, the so-called Three Dynasties, when China was believed to have enjoyed exemplary eras of peace and social order. He was especially interested, it would seem, in the rites, music, and other cultural elements that distinguished these periods.

Confucius's ambition, it would appear, was to gain official position in his native state of Lu so that he could put his ideals on morality and good government into practice. Later legend depicts him as, in fact, holding fairly high public office in Lu, but there is little or no evidence in the *Analects* to support such a supposition. To understand the problems that Confucius faced in his search for office, we must review the social and political situation in the China of his time.

The Zhou people, founders of the dynasty under which Confucius lived, came originally from a region in western China. Kings Wen and Wu, who founded the dynasty, probably around 1040 B.C.E., had their capital in the area of present-day Xi'an. Under their rule and that of their immediate successors, China was divided into a vast number of feudal domains whose leaders acknowledged fealty to the Zhou king (or Son of Heaven) and aided him in repelling the attacks of non-Chinese peoples living on China's borders. One such attack in 771 B.C.E., however, forced the Zhou rulers to abandon their original capital in the west and move east to the area of Luoyang, a step that marked the beginning of the era known as Eastern Zhou (771–256 B.C.E.).

By this time, the Zhou kings had ceased to wield any real authority but were allowed to continue occupying the throne because of their religious significance as heads of the ruling clan. Actual power had meanwhile passed into the hands of the rulers of the larger feudal states, such as Qi on the Shandong Peninsula and Jin in northeastern China. In the *Analects*, Confucius is depicted as speaking favorably of the leaders of these two states because of their ability, at least for a time, to restore order and unity to the nation and protect it from foreign invasion.

Because the Zhou kings were no longer strong enough to enforce conditions of order and stability, as they supposedly had in earlier centuries, the more powerful feudal states were able to swallow up their weaker neighbors and ally themselves with one another to advance their aims. Thus the era was marked by almost constant warfare, the feudal lords, who lived in walled cities, venturing forth in cumbersome war chariots to attack this or that foe, accompanied by foot soldiers enlisted from the peasantry, who ran alongside the chariots. Confucius himself disclaimed any knowledge of military matters and deplored the warlike tenor of the age, but it is reflected in numerous passages of the *Analects*.

In addition to the threat of incursion from predatory neighbors, many of the feudal domains of the time were troubled by succession disputes. Although the principle of primogeniture was recognized in general, rulers at times disregarded it or delayed making clear their choice of an heir. Sons of the ruler, often by different mothers, vied for favor or fled or were exiled from the state entirely, taking up residence in neighboring states where they could gather supporters and, in time, attempt to enforce their claim to rulership. Such a situation is reflected in the *Analects* in the power struggle that ensued after the death of Duke Ling of the state of Wei between his son Kuai Kui and his grandson Che, a struggle in which one of Confucius's leading disciples, Zilu, was killed in combat.

The ruling family of Confucius's native state of Lu traced its descent to Dan, the duke of Zhou, a younger brother of King Wu, the founder of the Zhou dynasty. It was thus of ancient and distinguished lineage, and Confucius looked on the duke of Zhou with particular awe and veneration. But by Confucius's time, the dukes of Lu had lost much of their actual power and authority. As had happened or was in the process of happening in other states, power had passed into the hands of ministerial families — in Lu, three cadet families descended from sons of Duke Huan of Lu and referred to in the *Analects* as the "three Ji families." Powerful ministerial families such as these at times posed a serious threat to the rulers of the feudal domains and, in some cases, eventually overthrew and replaced them or brought about the partitioning of the states.

These, then, were the political conditions that confronted Confucius while he was growing up in Lu and acquiring the knowledge of Chinese history, culture, and ritual practice that allowed him to become a distinguished teacher. Because of such knowledge and his status as a member of the lower aristocracy, he was permitted to take part in rituals of the ruler's court and, judging from the *Analects*, was at times consulted by the ruler on matters of government. But, as stated earlier, it is doubtful that he ever held a government post of any distinction.

Meanwhile, he gathered around him a number of disciples, some of whom held posts in the service of the Ji families, and these he endeavored to imbue with his standards of moral conduct and political ideals. Failing to gain a hearing from the dukes of Lu, in his middle years he journeyed, together with some of his disciples, to nearby states in the hope of finding a more sympathetic reception for his ideas. But such wanderings proved for the most part disappointing and, at times, even exposed him and his followers to hardship and hostility.

His political ambitions unrealized, Confucius returned to Lu and devoted his remaining years to teaching. According to legend, in these later years he gave himself to the editing and transmission of the five so-called Confucian Classics, though in fact it is uncertain whether some of these texts were even in existence at this time.

According to the *Analects*, he had a daughter, whose marriage he arranged, and a son, Boyu, who died some years before his father. Confucius is said to have died in 479 B.C.E. In *Analects* 14:40, one contemporary of his, clearly not very favorably disposed toward him, describes him as "the one who knows there's nothing that can be done but keeps on trying." That may have been the general assessment of Confucius and his teaching at the time of his death.

The *Analects*

Lunyu means "Conversations," but the book is customarily referred to in English by the term *Analects*, which refers to a selection from the writings or sayings of a particular person — in this case, Confucius. It consists of a large number of brief passages, some only a sentence or two in length, arranged in twenty sections, or "Books." There appears to be little or no logic to the arrangement of the material. Many of the passages record sayings attributed to

Confucius, "the Master" ; others report the words of his disciples or describe historical incidents in which he or his followers figure, while a few passages seem to have little or no connection with Confucius at all.

Understanding of the work is made difficult by the fact that it is among the earliest extended prose works in Chinese and one that attempts to represent the conversational style of the period. It makes frequent use of parallelisms and the carefully balanced style typical of ancient Chinese and often cites rhymed "sayings" or lines of poetry to emphasize a point. At the same time, it employs a variety of particles that lend a conversational tone to the utterances.

It was probably a hundred years or more after the death of Confucius before the *Analects* assumed anything like its present form. Linguistic studies of the text and considerations of content suggest that some parts are of later date than others and that the text represents an amalgam of views held by different groups among the followers of the Confucian school. Readers interested in learning more about these theories regarding the dating of the different sections of the *Analects* may consult works such as E. Bruce Brooks and A. Taeko Brooks's *The Original Analects*. But for those encountering the text for the first time, it is best to read it as a unified whole and in its present order, which is how it has traditionally been read and understood over the centuries in China and the other countries within the Chinese cultural sphere.

The Chinese have shown a marked fondness for pithy sayings and the belief that the most important truths can best be expressed, or at least conveniently summed up, in aphoristic form, a conviction that clearly permeates the wording of the *Analects*. Moreover, they have believed, as evidenced by their abiding concern with the keeping and study of historical records, that ideas are best understood and remembered in the form of events tied to actual historical times and personages. In the *Analects*, therefore, the reader will find no lengthy discussions of terminology or expositions of ideas. Instead, moral and political concepts are presented in terms of particular individuals, the teacher Confucius and the disciple or other person with whom he is conversing, and the particular circumstances under discussion. And because the participants and circumstances vary in different passages, the manner in which the ideas are conveyed varies accordingly. The reader of the *Analects* should be prepared to encounter not a formal treatise but conversations that seek to illuminate or grapple with important concepts, sometimes in clear and succinct form, at other times in more oblique fashion, colored by the sort of surprise, misunderstanding, pleased reaction, displeased reaction, humor, or sarcasm that characterize conversations in real life. The *Analects* endeavors to present insights into the actual exchange of ideas between teacher and student, the activity that was at the core of Confucius's life and importance as an individual.

The Confucian Teachings

The best way to approach an overall discussion of the Confucian teachings as they are reflected in the *Analects* may be to examine some of the key terms that Confucius and his disciples employ in their pronouncements.

As stated earlier, we are not certain which texts and oral traditions were available to these persons to provide them with an understanding of early Chinese history. Confucius several times speaks of Yao and Shun, ideal sovereigns who were believed to have ruled the empire in very ancient times. Although the *Analects* makes no clear reference to the fact, Yao was traditionally believed to have passed over his own son and chosen Shun, a man of great virtue but unrelated to him by blood, as his successor. And Shun in time did likewise, it was said, ceding the throne to Yu, because of his moral worth, rather than to his own son. This "ceding" principle, the belief that wisdom and moral stature rather than birth alone are what qualify one for rulership, seems to underlie much of Confucius's thinking in the *Analects*. Nowhere does he actually advocate such acts of ceding or openly challenge the idea of hereditary rule. But in discussing the ruler's ministers, he makes clear that, in his view, it is moral standing rather than birth that qualifies one for official position; he stresses that in matters of education there should be no class distinctions; and he indicates that as a teacher he is ready to give instruction to anyone, regardless of the person's social background, who sincerely desires to learn.

According to legend, Shun's successor, Yu, the founder of the Xia dynasty, encouraged agriculture, carried out flood-control measures, and ensured peace and stability within the realm. His reign, and those of his immediate successors, like those of Yao and Shun, were models of good government. But in time, the virtue of the Xia rulers declined until the throne passed to Jie, an evil tyrant. At that point, at least according to later belief, Heaven (a term discussed later) withdrew its support, the so-called Mandate of Heaven, from the dynasty and bestowed it elsewhere. A virtuous leader, King Tang, arose to overthrow the Xia regime and found a new dynasty, the Shang or Yin, and once again China enjoyed wise and benevolent rule. The virtue of the new dynasty, however, followed the same pattern of decline, ending in the reign of another tyrant, Zhou (written with a different character from the name of the dynasty that supplanted him). Claiming that they were acting on the Mandate of Heaven, a new group of leaders emerged to challenge the Yin's rule: King Wen, the Cultured King, who began the undertaking, and his son King Wu, the Martial King, who overthrew the Yin, established a new dynasty, the Zhou, and initiated a new era of peace and upright government.

In the *Analects*, Confucius frequently employs the term *dao* (道), which means "a path or way" and, by extension, "a method of doing things." In some contexts, such as the writings of the Daoist school, the word has more metaphysical connotations. But in Confucius's pronouncements, it refers specifically to the characteristics of peaceful, benevolent, and culturally distinguished government typical of the periods of ideal rule, particularly that of the early years of the Zhou dynasty.

In the translation that follows, the word *dao* has usually been rendered as "the Way," with a capital "W" to signal its importance. Confucius gives various instructions on how to behave when "the Way prevails in the world" or when it does not. He clearly believed that it did not prevail in his time, as evidenced by the wars, usurpations of power, and departures from correct ritual practice that marked the age. But he also makes clear that he believes it can be restored at any time. China is not fated to suffer chaos and misrule. The common people are the same as those of the halcyon periods of the past; it is only the rulers who have gone astray. With a return to the principles of correct government, the Way can once more be made to prevail.

The ideal rulers of the past are customarily described as *sheng* (圣), or "sages," a term that occurs at times in the *Analects*. Confucius denied that he himself was a sage or that he had ever encountered a sage, though his compatriots in later centuries would dismiss these disclaimers as mere modesty.

If Confucius has little to say about sages, he spends a great deal of time describing those whom he calls the *junzi* (君子). The word originally meant "lord's child" and referred to offspring of the ruling elite. But Confucius, as we have seen, denied that birth alone entitled one to rulership and reinterpreted the term *junzi* to mean someone whose moral standards and superior understanding entitled him, if not to actual rulership, at least to high official position under a hereditary ruler. Other translators have rendered it as "gentleman," "superior man," or "noble person." I have translated it as "gentleman," with the understanding that the word here refers not to birth or class but to moral stature. That it refers to men and not women is clear from what we know of early Chinese society. Women had no legitimate role in politics and, in fact, make almost no appearance in the *Analects*.

Somewhat similar in meaning in the *Analects* is the term *shi*, mentioned earlier as a designation for the lowest level of the aristocracy. It is sometimes translated as "knight," since men of this class were permitted to ride in the war chariots and fight alongside the nobles of higher rank. Confucius, however, who belonged to the *shi* class, disclaims any knowledge of military affairs and places all emphasis on cultural and peaceful pursuits. When he uses the term *shi*, it seems to be virtually synonymous with *junzi*. I have translated it as "man of station," once more with the understanding that it refers primarily to moral stature rather than to class distinction alone.

Ancestor worship played a vital role in ancient China, and the *Analects* makes frequent mention of sacrifices and other rites performed for the spirits of the dead, as well as for nature deities of the mountains and rivers. Occasionally we find mention of a higher being or entity known as *tian* (天), translated here as "Heaven." The word may mean simply "sky" and refer to the impersonal forces of nature. More often, it seems to be a synonym for "fate" or "destiny," at times personalized, as when Confucius in a moment of deep grief exclaims, "Heaven is destroying me!" (11:9). Although Confucius speaks reverently of Heaven and the concept had profound significance for him, he has little to say about religious faith in general. In one famous passage, he advises one of his disciples to "respect the gods and spirits but keep them at a distance" (6:22). In trying to guess what he may have meant by this, one should keep in mind that Confucius's overriding concern was with the political conditions of his time and the degree to which they could be remedied by teaching people to pay stricter attention to moral standards. Rulers of the period, and of later eras in

Chinese history as well, were often greatly influenced by religious figures who claimed to be able to put them in contact with the spirit world or teach them the secrets of immortality. Confucius's attitude toward the supernatural was probably not agnostic, as has sometimes been claimed. But, as he said on another occasion, "When you don't yet know how to serve human beings, how can you serve the spirits?" (11:12). He wished first of all that his listeners would keep their attention focused on the ills of society.

As one might expect, the *Analects* abounds in terms designating the various ethical values that Confucius wished to encourage in the persons whom he addresses. Most of these, I hope, will be clear enough in meaning from the English renderings used for them in the translation: "trustworthiness," "courtesy," "respect," "reciprocity," and "loyalty," particularly in the sense of loyalty to another person's best interests. Special attention is given to rites, because it was believed that by performing the actions prescribed by ritual one could summon forth in the mind the emotions and attitudes appropriate to the occasion.

Readers might perhaps be surprised to observe the amount of emphasis on the term *xiao* (孝), or "filial obedience or devotion." But Chinese religion at this time, particularly among the upper classes, revolved mainly around veneration of the family ancestors, expressed through periodic sacrifices to them in an ancestral temple or at a family altar. Moreover, the family was envisioned as the inculcator of moral values in the young: one learned first how to pay proper respect to parents and ancestral spirits and how to live in harmony with siblings and other kin. Only after these patterns of behavior had been mastered in the circle of the family could they be extended to the other members of society.

One moral concept — in some respects the most important one in the *Analects* — poses considerable problems for both the translator and the reader. This is the principle referred to as *ren* (仁). It is written in Chinese with a character consisting of the elements for "person" and "two" and is pronounced the same way as the word for "person," allowing speakers at times to create puns based on this similarity. In order to make such puns understandable, and because I believe it to be the best choice, I have translated the term as "humane" when it is used as an adjective and as "humaneness" when in noun form. Other translators have rendered it variously as "benevolence," "supreme virtue," or "the Good."

Confucius employs the word *ren* frequently in his remarks, without ever clearly defining it. His disciples, puzzled, repeatedly question him about it, but he appears reluctant to discuss the term at length. Although numerous passages in the *Analects* refer to *ren*, the text at one point states: "The Master seldom spoke about ... humaneness" (9:11). This seeming anomaly is usually explained as resulting from the fact that, although the disciples were careful to preserve whatever comments the Master made on the subject of humaneness, they were dissatisfied that the sum of such comments was not greater.

At times, Confucius seems to imply that humaneness is quite close at hand, not that difficult to achieve; at other times, he pictures it as the loftiest of ideals and repeatedly denies that this or that person of his own time can be said to have achieved it. Perhaps he saw it as a kind of summation of all the other traits that he believed desirable in human relations, an ideal easily envisioned in the abstract, but impossible to achieve. Perhaps he believed that defining it too rigorously would only detract from its validity.

Probably because the *Analects* was compiled over a considerable period and represents the views of several different groups among the followers of the Confucian school, it is not always consistent in its presentation of the teachings. Some passages are of only historical interest; others are obscure in meaning or exasperatingly vague. But because Confucius's thinking centers mainly on questions of politics, education, and human relations, the vast majority of his pronouncements and those of his associates remain of vital interest to readers today. Indeed, the very vagueness of the wording has allowed the text to be reinterpreted or readily adapted to fit the changed circumstances of later ages — for example, by interpreting the term *junzi* to apply to women as well as men. As stated earlier, the *Analects* has in the past exercised a profound influence on the development of the culture of China and that of its immediate neighbors. One cannot hope to understand the history of those cultures without a knowledge of its contents. At the same time, it reflects not only a particular set of ideas that occupied one particular era of the past but an embodiment of sentiments and ideals that are relevant to all of human society. That is no doubt why the *Analects* has retained its validity for more than two thousand years and will continue to do so for the foreseeable future.

A Note on the Text and Interpretation

There are two main versions of the *Analects*: the Lu and Ku texts. They do not differ greatly, but I have noted in my translation one place where there is an important difference. The exact numbering of the individual passages differs slightly in different editions, and my own numbering may therefore not always coincide with that of other translations.

Commentaries fall into two groups: those dating from the Han and Six Dynasties periods, and later ones by Song dynasty Neo-Confucian scholars. My translation for the most part follows the interpretations that have been most commonly accepted over the centuries in China, the *Analects* as most readers in the past have known it. Where interpretations differ markedly and the differences are of significant interest, I have offered more than one translation of a passage.

In my translation, I have tried as much as possible to follow the wording and word order of the Chinese. The language of the translation, however, is in no way intended to reflect the antiquity of the text. It is in the colloquial English that would be used if these conversations took place today.

Confucius/孔子

Selections from *The Analects* (Part I)

Translated by Burton Watson

1.1

子曰：『學而時習之，不亦說乎？有朋自遠方來，不亦樂乎？人不知，而不慍，不亦君子乎？』

The Master said, Studying, and from time to time going over what you've learned — that's enjoyable, isn't it? To have a friend come from a long way off — that's a pleasure, isn't it? Others don't understand him, but he doesn't resent it — that's the true gentleman, isn't it?

1.3

子曰：『巧言令色，鮮矣仁。』

The Master said, Clever words and a pleasing countenance — little humaneness there!

1.14

子曰：『君子食無求飽，居無求安，敏於事而慎於言，就有道而正焉，可謂好學也已。』

The Master said, A gentleman when he eats doesn't try to stuff himself, when he chooses a dwelling is not overly concerned about comfort. He is attentive to affairs, careful of his words, and looks to those who have the Way to correct himself. He's the kind who can be called a lover of learning.

1.16

子曰：『不患人之不己知，患不知人也。』

The Master said, Don't worry about whether other people understand you. Worry about whether you understand other people.

2.4

子曰：『吾十有五而志於學，三十而立，四十而不惑，五十而知天命，六十而耳順，七十而從心所欲，不逾矩。』

The Master said, At fifteen I set my mind on learning; by thirty I had found my footing; at forty I was free of perplexities; by fifty I understood the will of Heaven; by sixty I learned to give ear to others; by seventy I could follow my heart's desires without overstepping the line.

2.7

子游問孝。子曰：『今之孝者，是謂能養。至於犬馬，皆能有養；不敬，何以別乎？』

Ziyou asked about filial devotion. The Master said, Nowadays it's taken to mean just seeing that one's parents get enough to eat. But we do that much for dogs or horses as well. If there is no reverence, how is it any different?

2.11

子曰：『溫故而知新，可以爲師矣。』

The Master said, Be thoroughly versed in the old, and understand the new — then you can be a teacher.

2.15

子曰：『學而不思則罔，思而不學則殆。』

The Master said, Learning without thought is pointless. Thought without learning is dangerous.

2.17

子曰：『由！誨女知之乎。知之爲知之，不知爲不知。是知也。』

The Master said, You (Zilu), shall I teach you what it means to know something? When you know, to know you know. When you don't know, to know you don't know. That's what knowing is.

3.15

子入太廟，每事問。或曰：『孰謂鄹人之子知禮乎？入太廟，每事問。』子聞之，曰：『是禮也。』

When the Master entered the Grand Temple, he asked questions about everything. Someone said, Who claims that this son of a man of Zou understands ritual? When he enters the Grand Temple he asks about everything! When the Master heard this, he said, Asking is part of the ritual.

3.20

子曰：『《關雎》，樂而不淫，哀而不傷。』

The Master said, The Guanju ode — joy, but not excessive; sadness, but not to the point of injury.

4.5

子曰：『富與貴，是人之所欲也；不以其道得之，不處也。貧與賤，是人之惡也；不以其道得之，不去也。君子去仁，惡乎成名？君子無終食之間違仁，造次必於是，顛沛必於是。』

The Master said, Wealth and eminence are what people desire, but if one can't get them by means that accord with the Way, one will not accept them. Poverty and low position are what people hate, but if one can't avoid them by means that accord with the Way, one will not reject them.

If the gentleman rejects humaneness, how can he be worthy of the name of gentleman? The gentleman never departs from humaneness even for the space of a meal — in confusion and distress he holds fast to it; stumbling, faltering, he holds fast to it.

4.8

子曰：『朝聞道，夕死可矣。』

The Master said, Hear the Way in the morning, and it won't matter if you die that evening.

4.16

子曰：『君子喻於義，小人喻於利。』

The Master said, The gentleman is alert to what is right. The petty man is alert to what is profitable.

4.17

子曰：『見賢思齊焉，見不賢而內自省也。』

The Master said, When you see a worthy person, think about how you can equal him. When you see an unworthy person, reflect on your own conduct.

4.19

子曰：『父母在，不遠游，游必有方。』

The Master said, While his father and mother are alive, a son should not go on distant journeys. If he travels, he must have a fixed destination.

4.21

子曰：『父母之年，不可不知也。一則以喜，一則以懼。』

The Master said, You must not be ignorant of the age of your father and mother! For one thing, it is a cause for rejoicing; for another, a cause for fear.

4.24

子曰：『君子欲訥於言而敏於行。』

The Master said, The gentleman desires to be hesitant in speech but prompt in action.

4.25

子曰：『德不孤，必有鄰。』

The Master said, Virtue is not alone. It invariably has neighbors.

5.10

宰予晝寢。子曰：『朽木不可雕也，糞土之牆不可杇也。於予與何誅？』子曰：『始吾於人也，聽其言而信其行；今吾於人也，聽其言而觀其行。於予與改是。』

Zai Yu (Zai Wo) was given to sleeping in the daytime. The Master said, Rotten wood can't be carved; a wall of stinking earth can't be troweled. What's the use of trying to reprimand Yu?

The Master said, At first, when it came to people, I listened to their words and trusted their conduct. Now, when it comes to people, I listen to their words and observe their conduct. It was Yu who brought about this change.

5.15

子貢問曰：『孔文子何以謂之「文」也？』子曰：『敏而好學，不恥下問，是以謂之「文」也。』

Zigong asked, Why was Kong Wenzi given the posthumous name Cultured (Wen) ?
The Master said, Clear-sighted and a lover of learning, he was not ashamed to ask questions of his inferiors. Therefore he was given the name Cultured.

5.20

季文子三思而後行。子聞之，曰：『再，斯可矣。』

Ji Wen Zi thought three times before he acted. When the Master heard of this, he said, Twice is enough.

5.26

顏淵季路侍。子曰：『盍各言爾志？』
子路曰：『願車馬衣輕裘與朋友共蔽之而無憾。』
顏淵曰：『願無伐善，無施勞。』
子路曰：『願聞子之志。』
子曰：『老者安之，朋友信之，少者懷之。』

Once, when Yan Yuan and Zilu were accompanying him, the Master said, Why doesn't each of you speak of your desires?
Zilu said, I wish that I and my friends could share the same carriages and horses, robes and furs, and never worry if we wore them out.
Yan Yuan said, I would like never to boast of what good points I have and never cause trouble to others.
Zilu said, I would like to hear the Master's desires.
The Master said, To free old people from worry, to be trustworthy toward my friends, and at all times solicitous of the young.

6.11

子曰：『賢哉，回也！一簞食，一瓢飲，在陋巷，人不堪其憂，回也不改其樂。賢哉，回也！』

The Master said, What a fine man Hui was! One container of rice, one dipperful of drink, living in a back alley — others couldn't have endured the gloom of it, but he never let it affect his happiness. What a fine man Hui was!

6.18

子曰：『質勝文則野，文勝質則史。文質彬彬，然後君子。』

The Master said, Where solid qualities outweigh refinement, you have rusticity. Where refinement outweighs solid qualities, you have the clerkly style. Refinement and solid qualities beautifully balanced — then you have the gentleman.

6.23

子曰：『知者樂水，仁者樂山。知者動，仁者靜。知者樂，仁者壽。』

The Master said, The wise delight in water; the humane delight in mountains. The wise move; the humane are still. The wise are happy; the humane live long.

7.2

子曰：『默而識之，學而不厭，誨人不倦，何有於我哉？』

The Master said, To be silent and understand, to learn without tiring, never to weary of teaching others — this much I can do.

7.3

子曰：『德之不修，學之不講，聞義不能徙，不善不能改，是吾憂也。』

The Master said, Virtue not sufficiently practiced, learning not sufficiently digested, to hear what is right and not be able to do it, to have shortcomings and not be able to remedy them — these are the things that I worry about.

7.6

子曰：『志於道，據於德，依於仁，游於藝。』

The Master said, Set your sights on the Way, base yourself on virtue, rely on humaneness, relax with the arts.

7.8

子曰：『不憤不啓，不悱不發。舉一隅不以三隅反，則不復也。』

The Master said, If they're not eager to learn, I don't enlighten them; if they're not struggling to put it into words, I don't assist them. I hold up one corner to show them, and if they can't come back with the other three, then I don't go on.

7.16

子曰：『飯疏食飲水，曲肱而枕之，樂亦在其中矣。不義而富且貴，於我如浮雲。』

The Master said, Eating simple food, drinking water, a bended arm for a pillow — there's happiness in these things too. Wealth and eminence gained by unrightful means are to me mere drifting clouds.

7.19

葉公問孔子於子路，子路不對。子曰：『女奚不曰，其爲人也，發憤忘食，樂以忘憂，不知老之將至云爾。』

The lord of She asked Zilu about Confucius, but Zilu did not reply. The Master said, Why didn't you tell him that he's the kind of person who in bursts of enthusiasm forgets to eat, in his delight forgets to worry, and doesn't even realize that old age is coming on?

7.22

子曰：『三人行，必有我師焉：擇其善者而從之，其不善者而改之。』

The Master said, When I walk with two others, I'm bound to find my teacher there. I single out their good points and pursue them, note their bad points and make my corrections.

7.25

子以四教：文，行，忠，信。

The Master taught four things: culture, behavior, loyalty, trustworthiness.

7.37

子曰：『君子坦蕩蕩，小人長戚戚。』

The Master said, The gentleman is composed, at peace with things. The petty man is constantly fretting, fretting.

8.13

子曰：『篤信好學，守死善道。危邦不入，亂邦不居。天下有道則見，無道則隱。邦有道，貧且賤焉，恥也。邦無道，富且貴焉，恥也。』

The Master said, Entirely trustworthy, a lover of learning, faithful until death, exemplar of the Way, he never enters a state where there is peril, never remains in a state where there is disorder. When the Way prevails in the world, he appears; when the Way is lacking, he retires. When the state follows the Way, being poor and lowly is a cause for shame. When the state is without the Way, being rich and eminent is a cause for shame.

8.14

子曰：『不在其位，不謀其政。』

The Master said, If one does not hold the position, one does not dictate the policies that go with it.

9.4

子絕四：毋意，毋必，毋固，毋我。

The Master observed four prohibitions: no willfulness, no obstinacy, no narrow-mindedness, no egotism.

9.11

顏淵喟然歎曰：『仰之彌高，鑽之彌堅。瞻之在前，忽焉在後。夫子循循然善誘人，搏我以文，約我以禮，欲罷不能。既竭吾才，如有所立卓爾。雖欲從之，末由也已。』

Yan Yuan, sighing, exclaimed, Look up and it's higher than ever, bore into it and it's harder still. I see it in front of me, then suddenly it's behind. Our Master — step by step, how skillfully he leads others along! He broadens me with culture, reins me in with ritual. I want to give up but cannot. Already he has exhausted my ability, yet I see him standing tall before me. But although I want to follow him, I've no way to do so.

9.17

子在川上曰：『逝者如斯夫！不舍晝夜。』

Standing by a stream, the Master said, It flows on like this — does it not? — never ceasing, day or night.

9.18

子曰：『吾未見好德如好色者也。』

The Master said, I have never seen the person who loved virtue the way he loved physical beauty.

9.23

子曰：「後生可畏，焉知來者之不如今也？四十、五十而無聞焉，斯亦不足畏也已。」

The Master said, Respect those younger than yourself. How do you know that the coming generation may not prove as good as our present one? But if a person lives to forty or fifty and hasn't been heard of, then he's no longer worthy of respect.

9.26

子曰：「三軍可奪師也，匹夫不可奪志也。」

The Master said, The Three Armies may be stripped of their commander, but even a simple commoner cannot be deprived of his will.

9.28

子曰：「歲寒，然後知松柏之後凋也。」

The Master said, When the year-end cold comes, then we know that the pine and cypress are the last to lose their leaves.

9.29

子曰：「知者不惑，仁者不憂，勇者不懼。」

The Master said, The wise are never perplexed; the humane, never anxious; the brave, never afraid.

Auntie Xu

Jiang Limin / 姜琍敏
Translated by Michael Day

When I think back on Auntie Xu, I can't help heaving a sigh. I think that's the best way to put it. We all go through ups and downs in life. We all take some bumps and scrapes. We all, whether born into palaces or peasants' huts, are destined to experience the full gamut of human emotion, from happiness to anger to grief to joy. But what Auntie Xu went through, that was really something else ...

When Auntie Xu was young, it wasn't that she was so far above us, like some Taoist immortal looking down from on high, but her beauty certainly set her apart. As evidence of this, I offer the fact that business at the Gongnong Noodle Shop near our home on Qijing Lane grew by leaps and bounds with Auntie Xu on staff. It was 1964 or so, and China had recently emerged from three long years of famine, and we were all hungry and we were all poor, as anyone who went through it remembers. On top of that, you couldn't do anything without vouchers. The people looked at the noodle shop with longing in their eyes, because you needed food vouchers to eat there, and with incomes so universally low, few could afford to do so. Back then, noodle shops served simple fare, usually just plain noodles, with a dollop of vegetables on top if you were lucky. Meat was still being rationed, and a little noodle shop couldn't get much. Anyway, the point is that back then, a simple bowl of noodles in soy sauce was a delicacy. And when Auntie Xu's father suffered a stroke, and she took his place at the noodle shop, it seemed to draw bigger crowds by the day. Why? I was a child then, yet to turn ten, but even I understood that she was the reason.

In those days, we lived across the lane from the noodle shop. Qijing Lane was long and narrow, and each day I awoke to the waiters' cries of "four bowls of noodles" or "one bowl with extra garlic, one with extra soup" echoing down its lengths. The fragrance of pork fat and garlic saturated the air, and even in my dreams I'd find myself smacking my lips. It was hard to muster up an appetite for the meals of rice porridge with dried radish we ate at home. In those days, we didn't have the money to eat noodles all the time. In the classical joke book *Gleanings from the Forests of Laughter*, a tightfisted father hangs a slab of dried fish from a rafter and tells his sons they can assuage their hunger just by looking at it, an idea that to me didn't sound so unreasonable. Like them, I'd often try to fill my belly with deep draughts of the fragrances that wafted through the window. Sometimes my father would send me out with an aluminum pot to collect noodles from the shop, mainly to satisfy the gluttony of us kids. It was my favorite chore.

Afterward I'd tuck into a fresh, fragrant bowl of noodles in soy sauce, and I'd get the chance to exchange a few words with Auntie Xu, so naturally enough, I relished the task.

I later learned that Auntie Xu was twelve years older than me. My mother was the one who said I should call her Auntie. When Auntie Xu was in her twenties, the whole neighborhood swooned for her, and though I was too young to understand what the fuss was about, I would turn my head with the others to take another look. To tell the truth, when my mom and dad weren't around, I'd stand on the bed and peer past the window ledge into the noodle shop across the way, where Auntie Xu sat selling noodle tokens. Though the light was dim, her eyes would flash when she smiled, warming my heart.

What made Auntie Xu so good-looking was her perfectly oval-shaped face, and her skin was white and soft, with a faint blush of scarlet beneath, so stunning I could hardly stand to look. The most perfect part of her was the tiny mole beside her nostril. As brother of billionaire businessman Xu Shihui said, a glossy apple without a single blemish is nowhere near as pleasing to the eye as an apple with a wormhole in it. And I never tired of seeing her smile. Her eyes were on the small side, but they would glisten with life as she asked me, a smile lighting her face, head tilted just so, "How many bowls of noodles today?" The look on her face is still fresh in my memory.

You might say Auntie Xu's life was a steep rise followed by a sharp drop, a parabola-shaped life. She shined with beauty and she burned out, charming people for a while before falling like the magnolias in spring. And when she fell, it was a dramatic, crushing fall — though she certainly put up a fight.

Why, you ask? To hear my mom tell it, she picked the wrong husband, a fateful misstep.

It's not that my mother was wrong, but I couldn't completely agree. You see, I had a history with Auntie Xu's husband. Before they were married, he was my teacher. After graduating from the local teachers' college, he came to work at the elementary school on Qijing Lane. Back then, around the time Auntie Xu first joined the noodle shop, I had just started fourth grade. And that's why, even as an adult, I always called him Mr. Luo.

I recall that there was a new gym teacher when school started that year. He had a thick mane of slicked-back hair, a big, square face, and a bulky frame, but he was on the short side, only 170 centimeters or so tall. This was Mr. Luo. Before long, instead of Mr. Luo, the kids took to calling him "Mr. It-Was-the-Wind" behind his back. When the boys in particular spoke of him, the color would drain from their faces, because he nearly never smiled in class, and when they slacked off or made mischief, he'd beat their rear ends with a basketball.

When Mr. Luo first came to the school, he especially loved teaching basketball, and when he demonstrated on the little court, he'd miss seven or eight out of ten shots. With each shot he missed, he'd sigh and click his tongue, saying, *it was the wind*. In spite of the wind, he wouldn't give up. When at last he managed to sink two shots in a row, he'd blow fiercely on his whistle: "Did you see that? That's how it's done!"

The girls, being the weaker sex, were left to play at whatever they wanted, kicking shuttlecock or jumping rope. The boys all lined up in single file, shooting baskets one after another, a single shot and on to the next.

To tell the truth, the foul line was too far away for a small child, and we hadn't practiced enough, so even though most of us made two-handed shots, the ball often failed to even hit the rim. When that happened, Mr. It-Was-the-Wind, without a single question as to the cause, including whether it was the wind, would haul you off the court. And if you missed too many times in a row, Mr. It-Was-the-Wind would grab a basketball and whack your rear end. At this point, no matter what the wind conditions, the ball never missed the target.

In spite of everything, I liked Mr. It-Was-the-Wind. I'd

gone through the same torment on the basketball court as everyone, but to me, Mr. It-Was-the-Wind was something of a mentor. In fifth grade, he began to select and train the most promising softball players. These days, for whatever reason, you don't hear much about students playing softball in gym class. Back then, at least where I lived, it was a very popular activity in elementary and middle schools. I suppose that's because it's an inexpensive, accessible sport, making it well-suited for the tight economic conditions of the time. In terms of size and weight, a softball is somewhere between a tennis ball and a shot-put, and the rules of the game are very simple. You just toss it like a shot-put. Anybody can do it. But in an actual game, things get more complicated. Like soldiers tossing grenades, there's a knack to it, and a set of rules to follow.

When it came to softball, Mr. It-Was-the-Wind had talent. He'd demonstrate for us, trotting to the mound, turning to the side, and raising an arm in a series of flowing motions, pitching beautifully nine out of ten times as the students oohed and ahed. After all, he had experience. They said that at the teachers' college, he'd won first place in thc district, and then third place in the city. So to him, the search for young disciples to continue his legacy was a serious matter.

As he combed through the student body for glimmers of talent, he happened upon me, an empty-headed boy whose favorite pastime was skimming stones on the canal, and I became the sole disciple of Mr. It-Was-the-Wind. His first goal was for me to come in first in the district's high school division and place third in the district overall, and as far as the city went, we'd cross that bridge when we came to it.

Mr. It-Was-the-Wind's training regimen for me was as follows: every day except Sunday, after class let out, I was to stay at school doing homework for an hour, then start practicing and keep at it until it got too dark to see. This posed a problem. Class generally let out at three or four, and by the time I'd done an hour of homework it was almost five, and if I practiced until dark it would be almost six. But I ate only rice with radish and cabbage for lunch, and by that time my stomach would grumble in protest. Not an ideal training regimen.

But Mr. It-Was-the-Wind had a solution. This is another reason why I've always liked him: before each practice session, I'd find waiting for me either a piping-hot *shaobing* bun from the pastry shop near the school gate, or a baked sweet potato fresh from the oven. If he'd spent the school's funds, that would have been one thing, but he paid with his personal money, and he never bought himself a snack. At first I couldn't resist the delicious fragrances tempting my nostrils, but I was also ashamed to monopolize these tokens of goodwill, especially when I glimpsed the hungry looks of the other students who had stayed late for some reason. But Mr. It-Was-the-Wind would lock eyes with me as if to say, I'm the coach, what I say goes.

I know very well that the reason Mr. It-Was-the-Wind didn't buy a snack for himself wasn't lack of hunger, but lack of funds. The students whispered that he was poor. Mr. It-Was-the-Wind's father had died young, and though his mother worked at a store as an accountant, raising four children alone was tough. Mr. It-Was-the-Wind had only recently started working, and he was the oldest child, so you can well imagine that his financial situation was a bit rocky. At the time, none of us students knew what it meant to struggle to feed a family, and we weren't under pressure to support ourselves like him, but it was obvious even to us that he was going through a rough spot. He smoked either Laodong or Albania cigarettes, and the stale stench of cheap tobacco trailed him for meters. No matter how sweaty he got in gym class, he never took off the jersey with the teachers' college logo, not only out of loyalty to his alma mater, but because, as one of my classmates noticed, the tank top he wore beneath was full of holes, and sometimes he wasn't even wearing it. The first thing Mr. It-Was-the-Wind did when we started our practice sessions was to take off the old pair of leather shoes he'd worn for as long as I'd known him. Sometimes, when he wasn't wearing his jersey, he'd take off the dickie beneath the jacket, then put the jacket back on. I realized then that either the shirt beneath was a threadbare rag, or he had nothing under the jacket but the dickie. He'd removed the dickie so it wouldn't get sweaty, but what about the shoes? To hear Mr. It-Was-the-Wind explain it, he could run better that way. But if you ask me, he was worried about wearing out the soles.

There's one other little thing I'll never forget.

One day, Mr. It-Was-the-Wind went to the city for some kind of meeting where they passed out bottles of soda to the attendees, and he brought his bottle back unopened. It was about the same size as a mini Coke bottle, but in those days a soda seemed so much more special than a Coke or a Sprite. Instead of popping the cap with a bottle opener, he twisted his neck and gnawed up the edge with his teeth, not expecting the torrent of foam that burst forth from within. Mr. It-Was-the-Wind hurriedly sucked at the spurting liquid, taking several swallows and yelling, "quick, quick," thrusting the bottle between my lips before I'd even gotten my mouth open. I'm lucky I made it through that with all my teeth.

Wiping the sweat from his brow, he flashed me a smile. "That was a close one. I didn't know it was so fizzy. But soda is pretty good, right? All light and bubbly." He smacked his lips, licked his chops like a child, peered up into the bottle and shook it, hoping to taste a last drop or two, but nothing came out. When he set down the bottle in chagrin, he found the last drops of liquid that had collected at the bottle's mouth now trickled down his arms, and he eagerly stretched out his tongue to lap them up.

During our coaching sessions, Mr. It-Was-the-Wind got a better workout than I did. The gym had only three softballs, either because the school had no money or because gym class just wasn't a priority. During the sessions, he'd analyze my movements and point out mistakes, then he'd have me pitch all three balls, after which he'd rush out bare-footed to gather them up. He'd give another round of analysis and advice, and again I'd pitch the balls. As he ran back and forth, his brow would bead with perspiration, and he would begin to pant. Once, during one of these bare-footed coaching sessions, he abruptly cried out in pain and slumped to the ground. One of the students had dropped an open pen knife on the ground, and it had sliced a giant gash into his foot. I watched the fresh blood gushing from the wound, and a chill ran through me as it occurred to me that this would be our final day of training. I couldn't have imagined that he'd blow into the wound, grimacing, spit a few dabs of saliva in it, wrap the injured foot with a handkerchief, and wave a hand at me: what are you looking at? Throw the ball!

I moved to collect the balls, but Mr. It-Was-the-Wind wouldn't allow it, and went to pick them up himself. The difference was that now he wore shoes, and he hobbled around, wearing a pained look.

This training began when I was in fifth grade, and went on for about three or four months before it was interrupted by an unexpected incident. Those few months meant a lot to me, not only because I got to know, better than any other student, what a conscientious, hardworking person he was, but also because I'd always lacked self-esteem, and they gave me a much-needed boost in confidence.

One Monday morning, I arrived to find the classroom buzzing with gossip. As the students whispered excitedly in one another's ears, the substitute teacher, Mr. Zhang, sternly berated them: "What's all this commotion? So you think it's funny, do you? Just remember, like teacher, like student. Laugh all you want, have a ball, sooner or later you'll end up like them!" I was then that I realized the gravity of what had happened. After class, I followed along and pressed in with the crowd toward the little storehouse and teachers' office behind the reception room. A teacher barred the door, forcefully waving the crowd away. The mob contained not only nearly all the school's students, but also many of the men and women who farmed the nearby fields. How they'd heard the news so quickly, I had no idea, but they'd surged into the school like it was a country fair. The truth was that none of us could see who was inside the little rooms behind the storeroom and the teachers' office. But rumor had it they were keeping Mr. It-Was-the-Wind in one room, and our homeroom teacher Mrs. Li in the other, and both of them were writing self-criticisms.

I felt an ache in my chest. I wasn't at all excited like my classmates were. Instead, I felt fear and a despair that chilled me to the bone. I pushed desperately forward, not to gawk, but to get a glimpse of Mr. It-Was-the-Wind and Mrs. Li for myself. The crowd's ridicule of them stabbed my heart like a steel needle.

On Sunday evening, tipped off by the fat old woman who guarded the school gate, the principal and several teachers had stormed onto the school grounds, broken into the building, and caught Mr. It-Was-the-Wind and Mrs. Li in the midst of an intimate encounter on the guard room cot. Because they couldn't produce a marriage certificate, the mob had locked them in the little rooms, where they'd spent the whole day writing self-criticisms, and that evening a school representative had hauled them off to the police station. The police confirmed they had committed no crime, and they were released. That evening, in a bamboo grove on the banks of the canal, the two of them tried to commit suicide by drinking fertilizer. Luckily, they were found and sent to the hospital.

I don't know what happened to Mr. It-Was-the-Wind and Mrs. Li went after that, but in any case, they both left the school. Still later, the Cultural Revolution began. Once, at a district-wide educational system criticism meeting, I found to my great surprise that Mr. It-Was-the-Wind, that is to say Mr. Luo, now commander-in-chief of the district's Culture and Education

Revolutionary Headquarters, was shouting from the stage in a vehement rebuke of the former leaders of the Bureau of Education and the schools. The principal of the elementary school on our very own Qijing Lane was among those strung up by the arms and subjected to a torrent of abuse by the crowd. But, two years later, it surprised me even more to learn that Mr. Luo and Auntie Xu were getting married. That day, with my own eyes, I saw a nearly new military jeep parked at the door to Auntie Xu's house, and then there was Mr. Luo, clad in a brand new Mao suit, a red flower pinned to his lapel, broad face bright white and cleanly shaven, beaming from ear to ear as he stepped out of the jeep. A crowd of admiring neighbors gathered around them, and Auntie Xu emerged, face scarlet, head low as he swept her away. Not long after, Auntie Xu disappeared from the noodle shop, and was rarely ever seen on Qijing Lane.

I learned only later that Mr. Luo was then serving as deputy director of the district's Revolutionary Committee, and that Mrs. Li, his partner in the tryst and the suicide attempt, had died a year or so later from the effects of the poison. Auntie Xu had caught his eye at the noodle shop on Qijing Lane where he was a regular client, and he'd gotten an introduction from a go-between. I don't know what Auntie Xu herself thought, but my mother and the other women of Qijing Lane tittered approvingly. She wasn't bad-looking, but after all she was the counter girl at a noodle shop, and on top of that her father was a small business owner, not an enviable political position in those chaotic times, so the deputy director of the Revolutionary Committee was an all-around amazing catch, and not long after they were married she quit the noodle shop and went to work as a clerk for the local roadway committee, later even serving as assistant supervisor of the commerce department — pretty fortunate, wouldn't you say? In those days everything was in short supply, and you needed vouchers to buy food and daily goods, and for larger items like watches and bicycles, you needed industrial product coupons, which were even more difficult to get. Not long after Auntie Xu went to work on the roadway committee, she was seen riding around on a brand new 26-inch Phoenix bicycle — and make no mistake, she had her husband's power and connections to thank for that. Auntie Xu lived a fortunate life, and thanks to her, fortune smiled on us, too. She and my mother had been friendly during her noodle shop days, and later on, when she ran into my mom, she'd slip her some vouchers for tofu or even meat. I'd found a girlfriend, and I wanted to buy a Shanghai brand watch, but we'd used up our industrial product coupons, so my mom asked Auntie Xu, and she got me one.

Life may not be an escalator to the stars, but we do expect things to generally get better over time, or at least stay stable. Nobody, anyway, wants a life like a climb to the top of a slide followed by a slippery ride to rock bottom. But what could Auntie Xu do? That's the hand she was dealt. Like they say, life is unpredictable, and we all go through our ups and downs.

Don't assume that Auntie Xu's sudden twist of fate originated from the turmoil sweeping through society. No. Though the end of the Cultural Revolution was a blow to both of them, especially Mr. Luo, it wasn't the fatal one. Because of his history in the Cultural Revolution, Mr. Luo was stripped of all his professional titles. Following a brief period of detention, they gave him back his career at the elementary school. Auntie Xu was also forced out of her job, but she stayed on the local roadway committee until retirement. In the end, the tremendous historical changes of the reform and opening-up period succeeded in "liberating" the people. In economic terms alone, Auntie Xu's family got a new lease on life. After so many years in the roadway committee's commerce department, Auntie Xu had come a long way from her noodle shop days, acquiring a superhuman business sense. Shortly after Auntie Xu turned 50 in the early 1990s, she went on unpaid leave and opened a dance hall with an attached teahouse in the district of the roadway committee where she worked. In those days dancing in public squares hadn't yet come into vogue, and urbanites who found themselves with a bit of leisure time danced ballroom, jitterbug, rumba, and other styles where they held each other tight, sometimes with the lights turned out. Auntie Xu's dance hall held six or seven sessions a night, each one extremely well-attended. Abandoning themselves to the flowing rhythms, young and old alike would forget their cares, lining Auntie Xu's pockets in the process. Once, after she'd had a few swigs of wine, Auntie Xu bragged to my mom that one year, at the peak of the madness, her income had hit a few hundred thousand RMB ...

By now I'm sure you understand that the cruel turn in Auntie Xu's life had nothing to do with money. And when my mother said her mistake was marrying the wrong man, she was right, in a way. As the saying goes, blame the father for the sins of the son. Though their son was the source of the trouble, there was no doubt its roots could be traced to Mr. Luo. Auntie Xu had gynecological problems, and it was only several years after their marriage that she gave birth to a son, Luo Xiaotian, nearly dying in the process from massive blood loss. From the name Xiaotian, which means "roaring skyward," you can see that they had great ambitions for their son. Mr. Luo made no secret of his conviction that if his family hadn't been dirt-poor in his youth, other people wouldn't have looked down on him as they did, and then he wouldn't have sunk into a depression, and then he wouldn't have sought revenge by joining a rebel faction, and so on ... in any event, he placed high-minded hopes on this son whose birth itself was already a miracle. Whatever other fathers did for their sons, he'd do too, and whatever they didn't do, he'd spare no effort to pull off. He realized only much later that he'd gone too far to the opposite extreme. As a result of being spoiled for years, not only did his son not "roar skyward" as he hoped, Luo Xiaotian lay around the house, wallowing in narcissism, roaring complaints, issuing commands, making no move to do anything in the outside world, a cowardly, cold infant emperor. Auntie Xu tried to nudge her son in a different direction, but his father always shielded him, and by the time the two of them finally saw eye to eye, it was much too late — their baby, Luo Xiaotian, had graduated from vocational school, and Mr. Luo pulled some strings to get him a job, but just two years later, they received terrible news. Luo Xiaotian said he was going on a business trip, and a few days after he left home, Auntie Xu received a call from her son's company, informing her that he'd been fired. The reason was that he'd slacked off at work and racked up enormous gambling debts. At first the two of them only half-believed, but that evening some men with green dragon tattoos paid them a visit. They announced they'd be bedding down on the floor until Luo Xiaotian returned to pay off his debts. Mr. Luo asked with apprehension, "How much does he owe you?" The answer was, "We'll waive the interest. Just pay us 700 thousand, and we'll leave."

Auntie Xu spent all day at the dance hall, where shady characters were common, and she understood precisely how much trouble her son was in. "Oh, my god," she heaved, slumping onto the couch where she moaned to herself, coming back to her senses only hours later.

Once they'd paid off their son's gambling debts, he returned home one night, head hung low. Mr. Luo was ashamed, and walked the other way rather than face his son, even though his son was the one who should have been embarrassed. Auntie Xu collapsed onto her knees with a thump and kowtowed three times to Luo Xiaotian, so deeply her head banged on the floor: "My beloved son, what's become of you? You've used up all our savings. Please say now you'll stop gambling. I won't get up until you say it ..."

Luo Xiaotian did seem determined to change his ways. For the first year or two, all went well. But less than a year after the wedding, late one night he and his wife started arguing, and she howled that she just couldn't go on like this, with Luo Xiaotian away from home at all hours, and sunk so deep in debt ... this time Mr. Luo rose to the occasion. While his daughter-in-law watched, wearing a look like the one he'd had when hit our butts with the basketball, he took hold of his briefcase and gave his son's rear end a swift whack. It was the wake-up call he needed, and he made a clean break with his gambling friends. Or maybe you could say that the lottery, which was just getting popular then, was what saved him. He started playing the lottery, but it never got as bad as his gambling obsession. Thanks to his family's patient persuasion, he kept his habit under control. There was a whiff of mania to his behavior, as when he'd meet someone and immediately ask for their home and cell phone numbers, then mutter under his breath as he calculated their lucky digits. On the streets, other guys noticed girls, or the clothes people wore, but he was always craning his head to look at the numbers on the lampposts and the houses, saying he was gathering inspiration ... but Auntie Xu was convinced that playing the lottery was a lot better than gambling, so she'd slip him 2000 RMB a month for lottery tickets, under the condition that that was all he got to spend.

Not only did her son keep his end of the bargain, he fulfilled another of her wishes by making Auntie Xu a grandma.

Her grandson was growing bigger by the day, and he was a sweet talker. He clung to Auntie Xu especially, calling out grandma this, grandma that, and these cries seemed to restore a long-departed red glow to her sallow cheeks. Auntie Xu even talked to Mr. Luo, and they agreed to give their grandson the deed to the little apartment they'd been allotted after her childhood home on Qijing Lane was torn down. When her grandson was seven, she was taken aback when one of the dance hall regulars said this: "That little grandson of yours sure is a cutie! Especially his curly hair — it's just adorable.

So he must get it from your son?" Something clicked into place then, and the grin that spread wide across her face vanished like smoke, and her brow locked into a deep furrow that didn't release for days.

The customer's words had touched a sore spot. She'd met the department chair at her daughter-in-law's company, Mr. Qian, and her rapidly maturing grandson's curly head of hair was looking more and more like his. Auntie Xu had had a premonition that all was not well, but she chalked it up to being a worrywart, and managed to quash the kooky ideas that kept filling her head. But this time she was really worked up, and she sprang to action. Without telling Mr. Luo, through a mix of intimidation and enticement, she persuaded her son to agree with her plan to spirit away her grandson and get his blood drawn. The result was like a desolate northern wind that clawed away the final shreds of hope to which she clung.

Chaos roiled through the family. Their daughter-in-law had clearly seen it coming, and she was the one to propose divorce. But their son, Luo Xiaotian, hemmed and hawed and sniveled and whined, saying it was all his fault for getting involved in gambling, and he didn't want a divorce. The worst part was the "grandson" who'd grown up clinging to granny — how was it that he understood so much? When he heard his mother mention moving away with him, he held on for dear life to Auntie Xu's leg, crying and wailing and beating with his little fists: "Grandma, you lied! Grandma, lying is bad! You told me so many times, you said I'd always be your sweet boy, your little cupcake ..."

Auntie Xu had always been a softy. She thought about letting it all go, but these words from Mr. Luo hardened her heart: "No, they can't stay married. We can't let them cut off the Luo family line."

In the end, their daughter-in-law left, taking their "grandson" with her. But after many sleepless nights, over complaining by Mr. Luo, with a trembling hand Auntie Xu passed the deed in the name of her "grandson" to the boy's mother.

But the deed was nothing in comparison with what she would lose next.

Two or three cold, lonely years passed, relatively peaceful years, and at last there were glimmers of hope — Luo Xiaotian remarried, and shortly after, his new wife got pregnant. This time, an ultrasound revealed that the baby was a girl. When Mr. Luo and Auntie Xu thought of their lively, quick-witted little "grandson," they were just a tad disappointed, but they came around quickly. Let it be a girl, then. Our very own adorable grandbaby girl is certainly better than a boy who's someone else's flesh and blood.

Neither Auntie Xu nor my family nor anyone else who knew her could tell you what sin she'd committed in a past life to deserve such torment. The two incidents that followed were like twin knives of fate that flew down from heaven and sliced off Auntie Xu's limbs — no, they chopped out her heart and diced it to bloody bits.

That day, Auntie Xu was at the teahouse when her cellphone rang, with a ringtone from her favorite Shaoxing opera. Like always, she paused for a moment to enjoy the music before picking up the phone, and a voice roared into her ear, jolting her like thunder: "Why did you take so long to pick up? Drop everything and hurry home. Now. You'll find out why when you get here. Don't waste time!" She nearly swooned at the urgency in Luo Xiaotian's tone. But when she arrived home, clutching her pounding chest, and saw the chaotic scene, she didn't know whether to be angry or afraid ...

Their son had found Mr. Luo hanging in the bedroom. There was a suicide note in his pocket addressed to Auntie Xu: "I no longer want to live, and I lack the strength to tell you, and if I keep on living I'll be a burden on everyone ... pull me down from here and burn me, and dump my ashes in the gutter, the sooner the better ... you should go get a blood test, too. May heaven watch over you ..."

Fortunately, the test showed she was fine. But really, how could she not be? They hadn't even slept together for two or three years. But anger and regret consumed her when she realized that if she hadn't opened that damn dance hall, Mr. Luo would never have infected himself with this shameful disease — AIDS.

To tell the truth, she'd seen Mr. Luo mingling in the dance hall, the life of the party, and she'd had some misgivings. Maybe she'd grown complacent, but he was over sixty after all, and no girl would give him the time of day, she thought, so she turned her head and let him do what he wanted. How could she have known her dear old husband would contract this unspeakable ailment?

On the one hand she felt her life was shattered, but on the other hand she was nearly seventy, so there was no point wallowing in misery. Auntie Xu sold the dance hall and the teahouse, figuring that since she still had about a million RMB and a big house, she'd just live like a recluse from now on, and get ready to care for her granddaughter — but then, when she thought of her granddaughter, again her heartbeat quickened, and refused to slow down. There were things about her son and his wife that sent up red flags.

Auntie Xu lived in a 120 square meter house with four rooms, with the study and the bedroom reserved for her son and his wife. As soon as they returned home from work, they retreated to separate rooms, where each surfed the net in solitude. That was what rubbed her the wrong way, what she couldn't quite let go. Her son had met his new wife online, and they weren't acting like a proper married couple, what with each of them on the internet all day long. If her worst fears were true... Auntie Xu also noticed that her son and his wife didn't often go out together. And each seemed to spend two or three nights a week away from home, going out separately. What the hell were they up to?

Once, in the wee hours of the morning, Auntie Xu was on the way to the bathroom when she glimpsed the light still shining in her son's room, and she couldn't stop herself from lightly trying the door, which he'd forgotten to lock. Auntie Xu wished later on she could un-see it, but the sight was burned into her brain:

Luo Xiaotian faced the fluorescent computer screen, as naked as the day he was born, chatting with another woman who, like him, wore nothing but her birthday suit.

Considering what the family had already been through, she couldn't imagine her son playing dad to another man's child for a second time, but before her daughter-in-law gave birth, she laid her cards on the table: "As soon as the doctor says it's okay to draw blood, go with her and get a test. If it says you're the father, I'll give the two of you 300,000 RMB to compensate for the trouble. But if not... I'm sorry, but you'll have to immediately get divorced, or get the hell out of my house!" Luo Xiaotian fished out a cigarette and took a despondent drag. After a long time, he responded sheepishly, "To tell the truth, it probably isn't mine."

"What? Dammit, son! Please tell me you're kidding!"

"When I count the days, it almost couldn't be."

Her son turned out to be right. The paternity test showed again that the baby girl wasn't his. This time, they wasted no time arguing. Luo Xiaotian himself said he had no feelings for his wife, and he'd just found a random girl online to make his mom and dad happy. He hadn't realized she was already in an affair with a married man ...

Auntie Xu's son and his wife had a peaceful divorce, and he solemnly informed his mother that that was the last damn time he was getting married. Luo Xiaotian said that three years ago, and true to his word, he has remained single.

"A ceaseless drizzle on a dreary Tomb-Sweeping Day" — the early April weather was just like Tang dynasty poet Du Mu described it. But this year there was something exceptional about the rain. As in the summer rainy season, the air itself seemed waterlogged. The drizzle flowed endlessly, and from time to time a mushy sun ray emerged from a black cloud, seeming to cast an even deeper gloom over the desolate graveyard. Tendrils of pungent smoke wafted from the flames that burned in little clusters where spirit money had been set ablaze, choking the air so that you could barely breathe. But to my surprise, as I finished sweeping the grave and went to help my mother down the hill, my eye suddenly alighted on a shriveled old woman hobbling along alone, pausing for a gasp of air after nearly every step. Age had swollen the contours of her face, but it still had a recognizable oval shape, and the tiny mole by her nose left no doubt — it was Auntie Xu. Head hung low, she gasped for air as she ascended, and she didn't catch sight of us. A bouquet of flowers peeked out from the bulging cotton sack in her hand. Surely she'd also brought along offerings of food and spirit money to burn for the dead.

I asked my mom if she'd seen Auntie Xu, and she looked up, face suddenly ashen, and pulled me down a forking path where we stayed until Auntie Xu passed by. I asked her why, and as she wistfully watched Auntie Xu recede into the distance, she said softly, "I don't want to embarrass her. I know her parents' graves are on the southern hill, so she must be here to visit Mr. Luo's grave. But she told me again and again she dumped his ashes into the gutter like garbage."

I couldn't help heaving a sigh. I asked my mother if she knew what Auntie Xu had been up to. Shaking her head, she said she knew a little. One time Luo Xiaotian had called her, begging her to talk some sense into Auntie Xu, saying she was acting weird. She obviously had money, so there was no way to explain it except that she was cracking up. Every evening, after dark, she'd make the rounds of the neighborhood's garbage cans, picking out the nice pieces of cardboard and bringing them home. But instead of selling them, she piled them on the veranda. He'd forced her to dispose of part of the collection, but she'd gone out and gathered more, so much you barely find a place to plant your feet, and the stench of mold had grown unbearable. The worst part was that sometimes, after taking out the trash, she'd bring the trash bag home and reuse it. And that wasn't all. Luo Xiaotian had hired a maid to cook for her. At first she wouldn't have it, saying it was a waste of money. Luo Xiaotian had absolutely insisted, but each time the maid left, Auntie Xu would count the plates and bowls in the kitchen, as if she suspected the maid was stealing them. And she'd stuffed some gilt-edged plates inside a quilt and crammed it in a cabinet. Yet the thought of someone stealing the two antique vases in the bookcase apparently hadn't occurred to her ...

"But at least now she and Luo Xiaotian are getting along?"

"No. I went to see Auntie Xu last month, and she said she'd had an attorney draw up a will. She sent a copy to Community Director Ding. It said that after she died, all her money and her house would temporarily be managed by the community. If her son got married within three years, and had a child, and the child passed a paternity test, proving it was Luo family flesh and blood, Luo Xiaotian would inherit all her assets. Otherwise, everything would go to charity ..."

I was struck by the sudden urge to see with my own eyes whose grave Auntie Xu was visiting. So I turned back and stealthily followed until she squatted before a tombstone and laid out the offering, muttering something unintelligible.

I tiptoed through the row of tombs behind her and peered through the branches of a cypress tree. If it wasn't Mr. Luo's grave, whose was it?

There were two graves side by side. On the tombstone, the name of Mr. Luo was written in black, and in red, the name of Auntie Xu.

2015

On the Plateau

Hu Xuewen / 胡学文
Translated by Kay McLeod

1

Hu Xuewen / 胡学文

He finally got a taste of the weather up in the highlands. The noonday sun was baking hot, then in the afternoon a squall of rain fell and the temperature dropped steeply. Wearing short sleeves, Mi Gao couldn't help but shiver in the chill. He did have his coat with him, but there was no time now to go back to the hotel. The spicy soup stalls on the roadside emitted puffs of steam. Mi Gao glanced absently over, and the stallholder quickly asked if he'd like a bowl. Mi Gao hesitated for a moment, then nodded. Normally he never ate this stuff. He didn't eat anything spread out in the open air, like barbecue or fried pancakes or the like — even to eat a bowl of noodles, he still had to find a little restaurant. It's not that he was fussy, and there was no particular reason, such as hygiene — small restaurants weren't exactly clean, either. It was just a habit.

Mi Gao sat down and, intentionally or not, squinted at the school gates. The food stalls were twenty-odd meters from the entrance, and though it wasn't yet home-time there were already parents gathering outside the gates, come to collect their children. This sight was no different from the primary schools in the city, apart from the vehicles doing the collecting: the usual cars were hemmed in by electric scooters, bicycles, and tricycles of every shape and color. When he'd eaten two seaweed kebabs, the noise was already greater, and Mi Gao's line of sight was blocked by legs and vehicles. He stood up hurriedly and squeezed forward, wiping his mouth. Suddenly he stopped. He had spotted her. She always fought her way to the very front, just an arm's length from the gates. He could only see her in profile but he could still sense her attentiveness, her anxiousness. For those other parents craning their necks was just a formality, but not for her. She never made small talk, and didn't even seem to hear what those around her were saying. It was as though the person she was collecting was not in a classroom, but returning from a distant planet. Mi Gao had observed her for three days now, and her demeanor was almost unchanging.

The gatekeeper opened the gates just as the school bell rang. The parents crowding outside the school entrance split conscientiously into two lines to leave a passage through the middle. Mi Gao pressed forward a bit until he could clearly see her face. She was wearing a deep purple top, which made her face look somewhat dull. In her hand she was clutching a small jacket, a pink one. She suddenly raised her other hand and beckoned — another troop of students had emerged. Mi Gao didn't know how she was able to distinguish her daughter from among them, all in uniform. She pulled her expertly from the procession, nimbly slipped on her coat, and squeezed her out and away. Her gaze was not intently focused as before, rather, it was now a little more ... vigilant. Yes, vigilant — her eyes darting from left to right. Mi Gao's gaze collided with hers for the first time. He let his immediately slip away, pretending just to be looking for someone. When he turned back, she and the girl had already walked to the other side of the road. Her electric scooter was there.

The school entrance was empty and the food stalls left one by one, but Mi Gao still stood there as if forgetting the bitter cold. She had seen him — she may not know him, but she had seen him, after all. She'd taken him for a parent, or maybe ... maybe she simply hadn't noticed him. So many faces, and there was nothing particular about him. That momentary collision of eye contact could very well have been just his imagination. But Mi Gao was still a little unnerved. There was really no need to come and wait at the school gate any more. He'd checked that yesterday, and he trusted himself. No need to come. He came again. Why must he come? He didn't reproach himself, just felt unnerved; unnerved, and an aimless emptiness.

Mi Gao finally turned back when the sky darkened. It wasn't a big town and it was cut in two by a narrow river, one hour's trip from east to west. There were five primary schools in all, as Mi Gao had determined on the first day. The girl's primary school was on the edge of the town, a bit remote, perhaps a deliberate choice by the woman. She must have moved to a lot of new places in the last few years, though of course she might also have hidden in this small highland town all along.

Mi Gao returned to the hotel and put on his coat, then ordered two courses and a bowl of rice at the restaurant just by the entrance. The dishes he ordered were the waitress's recommendation: fried bracken fronds and fried daylilies, both local specialties. They were indeed delicious. Mi Gao searched for the right words to praise them while the waitress watched him earnestly, as if waiting for confirmation that she hadn't duped him. His teeth bit something hard. It was a piece of grit. Mi Gao involuntarily touched his cheeks and spat it into his paper napkin, then rinsed his mouth. Seeing this, the waitress was a little nervous. Without saying a word, Mi Gao thought: if anything else crunches I won't spare any feelings. He didn't slow down his chewing — on the contrary, he sped up, as though intent on finding more hard bits. He ate up both dishes till the plates were clean, feeling full to bursting. Nonetheless, he strolled over to the alley where Fengfeng's Barber Shop stood. "Fengfeng" bore no relation to the woman's name, and the barber shop was a bit secluded. The woman and her daughter lived right there in the shop, which was closed at night — not like the usual hairdresser's on the high street. Now, all Mi Gao could see was lamplight seeping from the window. There was even less need to come to the alleyway. Mi Gao couldn't be sure, maybe it was the emptiness in his heart. His stomach was full and swollen, but his heart was emptier. He walked up and down a few times and at first he still saw people coming and going; later, only his own lonely shadow was left in the whole alleyway.

It was nearly ten o'clock when he got back to the hotel. He felt unwell in the shower. It wasn't just his heart that was empty: his whole body was empty. He reeled, then very cautiously leaned himself against the wall for a moment, gasping. The showerhead was still spraying water, with a sound like waves. On his first day in the hotel, he had sensed his body's reaction. He'd thought it was the effect of the altitude: two-thousand-odd above sea level, not a patch on Tibet, but still pretty high. He'd sleep it off and recover in the morning; it wasn't Tibet, after all. A one-off reaction would do the body no harm, but this was more like ... something flashed passed his mind's eye, but in his emptiness he couldn't quite grasp on to it. The sound of waves grew louder and louder. He reached out an arm and gropingly turned off the water. The sound of waves continued endlessly. Finally he realized that it was not altitude sickness attacking him. He paused again for a while, then rubbed his face, hard. He came out, steadying himself on the wall. He lay down for a while, and the motley sounds gradually died down. The dizziness was gone, but now another sort of panic attacked him. After all these years, he thought he would never have this suffocating feeling again. What was going on?

He had set the ringtone himself, an old tune which he heard countless times each day. But when it struck up in the depths of night it still seemed piercingly alien. In fact, he wasn't even asleep yet. It was the weekend, and near the end of the month — the call would surely come. Nearly a year had passed, and he'd already sussed out the routine of the phone calls.

"Where are you?" A hoarse voice, exuding a brusque ferocity.

"Guyuan." He paused and then added, "a little town up on the plateau."

"Guyuan?" Clearly, this was completely new to him. He had no way of imagining it.

Mi Gao said, "Near the Inner Mongolian border."

The man said, "Any news?"

Mi Gao looked at the wall, empty and bare, completely unadorned, and then he said: "Nothing yet."

The man said, "Next month's money has already been transferred to you."

The man didn't have much to say, and all his meaning was couched in terms of payments. Mi Gao knew it wasn't just about that.

"I got it." Whenever he hung up, Mi Gao always felt a violent resentment, as though the man had forced him to sign a life-or-death contract.

2

"Why are you hiding from me?" Xu Lili unflinchingly, unerringly interrogated him. Mi Gao's answers all followed the same pattern. "Why can't I see you? Where are you? I want to see you right now!" she'd yell. Mi Gao would say "I'm away, now's not a good time." Xu Lili wouldn't give up. "Where's 'away'? It could be Mars and I'd still want to go." Mi Gao would say "No, you can't come." Xu Lili would start howling, "You ARE hiding from me!" Mi Gao would say "Fine, but even if I am, we can't see each other." "You're such a fucking scumbag!" Xu Lili would end up hysterical. This was her endgame. Mi Gao would hang up.

Unlike the man's phone calls, Xu Lili's calls came at all hours — the crack of dawn, high noon, the middle of the night, as though she were thinking of Mi Gao every waking moment, as though he were her air and she couldn't live without him. Sometimes she stubbornly rang him again after he'd heartlessly hung up and he'd have to answer to spare himself the hassle. It would still be the same words with no change in tone. After many such encounters Mi Gao stopped answering her calls, so she started frantically sending text messages. Sometimes he would send a quick reply, but in most cases he ignored them.

Of course there would always be some reason for him to reply, like when her questions had nothing to do with him. Such as: "My throat is hurting like crazy, I can't make a sound." He replied: "Get some throat sweets then, and drink plenty." It was all nonsense. She was rapidly approaching forty and it's not as though she didn't know what to do. But he had to go through the motions. His heart wasn't that steely yet. The next day she said she'd gone through two packets and it was even sorer, as though something was growing in her throat. He said it was "definitely strep throat, you'll need to go and be put on a drip!!!" He used exclamation marks for extra emphasis. She asked "are you serious?" He didn't reply. At this sort of juncture she'd concede — "all right, I'll go right now."

Mi Gao was staring vacantly out at Shandian Lake when he felt the buzzing in his trouser pocket. He had headed out here after seeing an advertising brochure for Guyuan — the lake was ten or fifteen kilometers from the town, and apparently there were over a hundred species of birds thriving there. Mi Gao liked birds; he'd even kept a pet thrush before. It had been a rather extravagant hobby for him back then, so his ex-ex-wife had said. After the thrush died, he hadn't kept another one. If he wanted to see birds he would go to the nearby lake or to the city park. Of course that was in his days off. Now he had heaps of time again. On days off the girl didn't have to go to school and the woman didn't have to bring or collect her, and Mi Gao had no need to go and wait at the school gates.

The lake's surface was vast, yet there were scarcely any birds. He had to peer out for a long time before he made out a few black dots on the lake's surface in the distance. Probably mallards. When he used to go out into the wilds to watch birds he would bring binoculars. Since he couldn't see them clearly, he might as well sit down — at least this place had birds.

His pocket buzzed again, and Mi Gao slowly pulled out his phone. No need to guess, because only Xu Lili would keep obsessing like this.

"I'm on my way back to Xi'an ... where are you?"

Mi Gao's fingers were a bit stiff. He typed "Oh" twice before sending it.

"My mother died."

"When?" asked Mi Gao, with a churning feeling.

"Last night, during the night. She was fine a few days ago. I'm motherless."

"Can I help with anything?" Mi Gao stared for a while, then deleted it letter by letter. "Condolences!" he typed.

Xu Lili didn't reply. Mi Gao waited a while and she still didn't reply. He raised his head: there seemed to be more black dots on the lake. He counted — there were indeed six more. The black dots were very far from one another, yet they were cognizant of each other's existence, just like ... just like he and Xu Lili were. This woman he was trying his hardest to hide from. Perhaps he could do something for her? Pondering this, he stood up. But what could he do? Appear suddenly by her side? Her parental home was in the outskirts of Xi'an, he knew that. On what basis could he just turn up? And what could he do? Mi Gao strolled up and down the dam a couple of times and sat down again. He decided to watch the birds, even if they were just a few black dots.

First he just felt faint, as though someone was covering his mouth and nose. Breathing became difficult and he had sharp pangs in his heart. Mi Gao was certain now that this had nothing to do with the thin air. This was an after-effect of his two marriages. He hadn't had a relapse for many years, and he'd thought he never would again. There was no shortage of women around him yet he had managed to steer clear of marriage: the firewall was working. He didn't know what was going on. He didn't shift his posture, just did his utmost to fight off the attacks of suffocating dizziness. After quarter of an hour or maybe half an hour he finally calmed down.

At lunch he ate a little something at the local inn on the shore of Shandian Lake, thinking of going back to the hotel yet with nothing to do there — better to stay by the lakeside. Bird-watching was as good a reason as any. Once he went back to the city he wouldn't see these high-altitude birds any more. "What about tomorrow?" a voice asked. Tomorrow I'll come and see the birds again. May as well watch them while I can — feed the habit. "And the day after tomorrow?" He furrowed his brows.

In the evening Mi Gao felt idle so he strolled over to the alleyway. Suddenly he heard the sound of howling. A very overweight woman ran into the alley with a man chasing behind her, neither of them running fast. The woman's arms were swinging and her legs flailing, while the man was staggering somewhat. They were seven or eight meters apart. In the end the man caught up and grabbed the woman, yanking her roughly, then suddenly letting her go. She sagged to the ground like a slack bundle, and rolled over a couple of times. The man took a few strides to straddle her and try to pull something from her chest. The woman held on for dear life with both hands and he, failing to force them open, slapped her in the face. The woman howled and yelled — "Robber! Robber!"

Four or five people quickly assembled nearby. They looked on, unmoved. Mi Gao was just about to step forward when an old woman said, "It's Old Three there beating his wife after a booze-up. Sooner or later someone's going to get killed." Mi Gao stopped in his tracks.

The man eventually got his way, and yanked out a small pouch from the woman's bosom. Presumably it was all that was left of their family belongings. The man rose and made as if to leave, when the woman suddenly pounced on him and pulled at his legs. Taken by surprise, the man tripped and fell flat on his face. All around him people roared with laughter. The woman part-rolled, part-crawled, pressing the man underneath her, and the cloth pouch returned once again into her grasp. By the time he staggered to his feet, she was already gone without trace. She hadn't gone far, just wound her way into the tofu shop opposite. Someone pointed in another direction and the man was off, grumbling and swearing.

Standing on the periphery, Mi Gao's attention had already moved to Fengfeng's Barber Shop. The woman must be able to hear the commotion in the alleyway, so surely she would at least stick her head out. But everyone was gone and the alley was empty, and the barber shop's door had stayed shut from beginning to end. The outside world had nothing to do with her; the barber shop had become a real fortress for her and her daughter.

3

In the lamplight the woman in the photo seemed a little ashen but without looking sickly at all. This had to do with her big eyes, so dark and deep, as though about to melt away at the lightest touch. The man had provided the photo, along with half a diary. The other half had evidently been torn away, its traces still visible. It was actually just an exercise book, mostly lines of poetry and a few inspirational stories, and occasionally a line of private secrets were recorded in the blank sections. "She kicked me just as I put down my pen;

suddenly I remembered last night's dream about running for my life on the plateau." It wasn't even a hundred words, all told. And what else? Anything she used, like an old phone or a comb, anything like that? The man shook his head and said they'd all been disposed of, and that because of the train station being relocated, the apartment where she'd lived had been demolished too.

That day was the Mid-Autumn Festival, and Mi Gao could have been the only person in the whole tower block. To avoid Xu Lili, he hadn't come down for a whole day. He received a call from an unknown number in the evening which he thought was Xu Lili — sometimes she would use other people's mobiles. He hesitated, then answered.

Half an hour later Mi Gao and the man were in a café. Mi Gao wanted some fresh air after being shut up inside all day. Of course the man's despairing tone had an effect as well — he was like a man on his deathbed entrusting Mi Gao with his final affairs, a mournful shrillness in his hoarse voice.

Mi Gao had taken on countless cases in recent years, and had met all kinds of strange unthinkable people and affairs. Sons suing fathers, mothers suing sons, mistresses suing first wives, illegitimate children bringing their biological fathers to court ... In legal circles, Mi Gao's nickname was "Gutsy Mi," he who dared to take on any case and file any lawsuit. Of course there were dangers. He had scars on his face and his head had been stitched up twice. His daughter was abroad and he was all alone; he didn't fear being roughed up. The lawsuit that made Mi Gao famous was one it took him three years to track down: he wound up locating a subcontractor with a fake name, as well as evidence that the subcontractor had been secretly transferring property. He'd recovered hundreds of thousands for those migrant workers.

No doubt this guy had some kind of suit to file, too. But when he'd pretty much finished talking, Mi Gao was a bit nonplussed. "I'm a lawyer,"

Mi Gao carefully pointed out. "There's no need to remind me," the guy said. Mi Gao told him to find a private detective, that he didn't take on this kind of work, that he couldn't do it anyway. The man said he'd employed six detectives and eight years had passed in vain. "Call the cops, then!" Mi Gao said. "The police are several times more effective than private detectives." The man said nothing. Mi Gao sensed his displeasure. Either he didn't want to report it, or he couldn't — Mi Gao could tell that without being told. Mi Gao said he really couldn't do it, that he should find someone better-qualified. He got up, planning to head off. The man suddenly seized Mi Gao. "I haven't finished. Sit for a while longer. Just a little while, okay?" Mi Gao had no choice but to sit down again. The man mentioned a very considerable fee. Mi Gao did not bat an eyelid, but faint ripples started moving in his chest. The man's adamant expression told Mi Gao with no room for doubt that this was exactly the price he would pay, and no mistake. The man added, "I only beg you not to get distracted." Mi Gao was silent for a moment, but still shook his head. The man made Mi Gao name his price. Mi Gao said slowly, "This isn't an issue of pay." The man's offer was very generous but it wasn't much of a temptation for Mi Gao. Although his money belt was hardly drooping with coin, it was enough for his daughter or even his granddaughters, to enjoy a fine life — not that she was buying private jets and private yachts. As for himself, he didn't need much, just three meals a day. These days he didn't take on cases for the money: it was a lifestyle for him. The man looked at Mi Gao, perplexed. Mi Gao had no desire to explain himself much, and he asked the man again to find someone better-qualified. The man said, "But *you're* better-qualified." Mi Gao denied it. The man's unmoving gaze fell, then suddenly flicked up again as he begged — "Please help me!" Mi Gao felt a sharp pain in his heart. A few years ago a woman had looked at him just as pitifully and begged him to help her to avenge her husband. Mi Gao hadn't taken that case because he'd already signed a contract with her family's opponent. Mi Gao won that case for his client, who only had to pay out the funeral expenses. But he wasn't the least bit light-hearted about it. For a long time, Mi Gao kept thinking about the woman's expression. Now it was this man. He'd had a domineering air about him a moment ago, yet now his face was caving in with sorrow. Mi Gao said, a little weakly, "All right, then."

The man swiftly opened his briefcase. A solid brick of banknotes with the bank's paper seal still on them. This was the deposit; he would transfer the rest to Mi Gao's bank account monthly. The agreement had been prepared well in advance and Mi Gao just had to sign it. Mi Gao flipped through it: there were no hidden clauses, so he signed it. The man packed away the agreement, his expression no longer so crumpled. "No need to call me, I'll call you!" Then he gave Mi Gao the photo and the half-diary.

Mi Gao thought afterwards that he probably signed the agreement with the man to challenge himself — no harm in a change of lifestyle, necessarily. That was the period when Xu Lili was hassling him and things were getting messy — just as well to hide out. Naturally the man had some kind of history with the woman — the man didn't say, but of course Mi Gao didn't have to ask. The ins and outs and rights and wrongs were hard to divine. But on top of that ... there just weren't enough clues.

"What about contact details for her old classmates, her friends?"

The man shook his head. "I'm not sure, she never told me."

Mi Gao's gaze returned to the photo. "And her family?"

The man furrowed his brow with a hint of impatience, as though he hadn't been begging Mi Gao for help, as though Mi Gao had been begging him.

Mi Gao began, "If you'd rather not ..."

After a long pause the man said, "She was an orphan."

4

The woman held her

daughter's hand as she always did, walked across the road, and unlocked her bike. She used a U-shaped lock and she usually locked the back wheel. In that very instant when she crouched down, a dark shadow flickered by and quickly bundled off her daughter. Before the woman had time to react, the shadow had run nearly twenty meters away. The woman took to her heels and made chase. Clutching the girl, the shadow slipped into a car parked on the road and was gone. The woman flung herself to the ground, howling in anguish.

Mi Gao awoke from the dream with a start, his throat burning. He felt for his slippers and poured a good half-glass of cold water. Looked at the time — not even four o'clock. He lay down again, but try as he might, he couldn't get back to sleep. He seemed to hear sobbing by his ear. Mi Gao stilled his breath and sure enough, it was coming from next door. There was a young couple next door, Mi Gao had seen them in the lift. The two of them made a racket most of the night, and Mi Gao at one stage had wanted to go and knock on the door. In the end he couldn't bring himself to do it. Who hasn't been young once upon a time?

He turned on his phone and a text from Xu Lili jumped out at him, just one word: "Cold." Sent two hours earlier. In August, the nights in Xi'an probably were a little chilly. But he knew that Xu Lili's "cold" had nothing to do with the temperature. She had to take sides between her two elder brothers. From her nonsensical message he caught a glimpse of the black hole of oppressive family politics. He didn't give her any suggestions. Family cases were plain sailing for him, yet in his own two marriages he'd been defeated twice. There were things much harder to resolve than just winning or losing. That is, unless he were her attorney — but due to their prior relationship, there was no chance of that. He would never be lawyer to his own. He hadn't even been in contact with Xu Lili for all that long, but in his mind, at least some of the time, he saw her as "his own." Mi Gao considered it for quite a while and then replied with three words: "I'm cold too." Suddenly he thought of the woman in the dream. She was colder than him and Xu Lili. Although he'd never scrutinized her eyes at close range, his observations of the last few days of her posture, her manner, the barber shop that became her fortress at night — everything about it exuded bitter cold and fear.

It was this kind of thing that gave Mi Gao cause for hesitation. All it needed was one phone call, and his task here would be finished completely. In the terms of the agreement there was one stipulation about a reward. Besides monthly payment, there would be additional incentives. But Mi Gao understood that the woman and her daughter's lives would be changed forever. He had no clear picture of the man's history with the woman and the girl, but he could make a rough guess at the basics. And although he wasn't clear on how the man would go about it, he knew that nobody spends years searching for a woman just for the sake of searching. Mi Gao didn't dare to follow that thought any further. Should he just keep going through the motions? Even if his search was fruitless, the man would still pay him as usual. That was very clear in the agreement. The man couldn't undo that clause, nor did he seem to want to. But that just led Mi Gao to a different kind of anxiety, one which had nothing to do with salary.

His head felt swollen and painful. After showering, Mi Gao wandered to the school entrance. There was already no need to lie in wait there, but Mi Gao couldn't help himself. Besides, he didn't know what else to do in that little highland town. He'd watched birds now for two days straight.

The food stalls were already setting up one by one. The earliest arrivals at the school were not the teachers, nor the pupils and parents, but that cluster of food stalls. Seeking a pretext, Mi Gao bought a breakfast pancake and clutched it in his hand. It wasn't as bustling as the end of the school day, so it was hard for Mi Gao to mingle into the crowd. He was afraid she would discover him. She'd probably noticed him. She looked no different to the other parents, but she was always secretly on the alert: that was her defensive weapon.

When the woman and her electric scooter entered his field of vision, Mi Gao actually felt a little nervous. The woman stopped and moved to lift her daughter down, but the girl didn't want her to. She pushed her mother away, apparently wanting to get down by herself. The woman said something, but in the end there was a compromise and she just made a protective gesture. The little girl skipped inside, in through the main gate, then she turned and waved towards the woman who was still standing in her original spot. The woman didn't leave straight away, and her gaze followed her daughter into the classroom.

It was deserted outside the school gates, and even the air was thinner. On his way back, Mi Gao gave the breakfast pancake to a street sweeper resting by the side of the road. She was a brown-faced woman who thanked Mi Gao about twenty times. This street was her assigned cleaning area. In the last few days with all his coming and going, Mi Gao had got to know all kinds of things that weren't his business. He thought of Yucai Street back in Shicheng, where his daughter went to the school at the corner of Yucai Street and Huaibei Road. After the divorce he was basically the only one who dropped off and collected his daughter. He didn't just learn the names of all the shops on either side of the road, he even got to know the smell of Yucai Street. His daughter's junior high school was a boarding school, and when she graduated from junior high school he sent her abroad. It wasn't so convenient to travel abroad, so he didn't go and see her. Whenever he missed his daughter he'd go and take a walk on Yucai Street. The shop names were constantly changing, but Yucai Street still had that particular smell. If he carried on like this, it would become his own Yucai Street. Walking on Yucai Street, he knew what he had to do; on this street up in the highlands, he'd already lost sight of purpose. It was more like being lost, or dreaming.

Reaching the bridge, Mi Gao stopped and leaned on the stone railings. The sky was spotless, cleansed. You never saw such a blue nor such a clear sky in Shicheng. That could be his reason to stay in the little highland town, or at least part of the reason. The sky up on the plateau was blue forever; he could stay here forever. If he wanted.

5

The day her mother was buried, Xu Lili left. She had planned to stay on a few days; her mother's spirit hadn't gone far yet, and could only be felt in the family home. But like two halves of a pair of scissors, her two brothers had her caught in between them so that leaning in any direction was unbearable, so she chose to escape. With her mother gone, home was no longer a home.

Like a highly skilled tailor with the finest needle and most delicate thread, Mi Gao could piece together Xu Lili's sparse words to form a picture. Just as she always said, he understood what she was talking about. From the day they first encountered each other, he became her tailor. Xu Lili was half-way good-looking, but that was certainly not why they were together. Back then, he was already making a name for himself, not short of money and obviously not short of women either. Marriage left him cold, but he was still infatuated with women. He favored one-night stands and never muddied the waters: at day-break each would go their own way, strangers to one another, their paths never to cross again. If there were especially strong feelings they'd leave each other a number, but they wouldn't become attached. Mi Gao was strict about this: he had a separate phone which always had a temporary number. He'd constantly change the SIM card to cut off all unnecessary contacts. It wasn't like he was some kind of expert ladies' man, he just wanted to keep any possible hassle and harassment at bay. So the women who slept with him didn't know who he was. Until he met Xu Lili. He was her solicitor. He would willingly swear to God that he had no designs on her. That would have crossed the line, would have been a big taboo. As a result all their interactions, listening to her getting everything off her chest, it was all extremely relaxed. He blamed that damned night in the torrential rain, when he was stuck at her place, waiting for the rain to stop. She suggested they drink some wine, and he nodded. Later no matter how hard he tried, he hadn't the faintest memory of how it all happened. He'd done his head in, trying to hide from Xu Lili. She hadn't threatened him, but she did want to be with him, which just happened to be Mi Gao's great fear. "The world may be big, but there aren't many people who can really talk." That's what Xu Lili had said, and it played a big part in why Mi Gao hadn't cut off contact while hiding from her.

"I want to cut my hair," Xu Lili said. Her luxuriant hair grew down to her waist — it would be an awful shame to cut it. She wasn't negotiating with him, but she was sure to listen if he had any suggestions. What suggestions could he give, though? That she keep it for him? The thought flashed suddenly into his mind: if Xu Lili was here, he could take her to Fengfeng's Barber Shop to have her hair cut. Could he let Xu Lili come, though? She would come, all he'd have to do was give her the address.

"I'm in ..." Mi Gao stared for a long time, then again deleted it bit by bit. Using Xu Lili like this was a bit too low. He wanted to go and have a look inside the woman and the girl's fortress. When the barber shop was open, he could go in. He'd be a customer. He was worried about startling her, afraid the castle walls would crumble. But he did really want to go. Just like going again and again to the school gates and waiting there, there was no need any more. But if he were accompanying Xu Lili while she had a haircut, that would be different. Xu Lili wanted it cut anyway, and was it any matter where she cut it?

They hadn't seen each other for nearly half a year; he knew where she was, but she didn't know his whereabouts. He could use this as an opportunity to see her. Here in this town up on the plateau.

In the end, he typed out a line of text.

6

Xu Lili arrived on the following evening. Mi Gao had calculated that it would take her at least two days to arrive, as the little town had no airport — unless Xu Lili could soar through the air. So the moment he saw Xu Lili he stood rooted to the spot, as if departed from his senses. Without waiting for him to react, Xu Lili flung herself upon him and clamped on to his shoulder with her teeth. At once firm and fierce, like a ravenous yet unhurried panther. Mi Gao pushed at her haphazardly. Xu Lili welded herself to him. He gritted his teeth. "Gentler … gentler!" Xu Lili loosened her bite, and just when Mi Gao released his breath she bit him on the other side. Not so fierce this time, but for longer. Mi Gao drew breath hoarsely but didn't call out. Then whether he pushed her or she enfolded him, they both fell onto the bed.

There was a whole lot of tossing and turning. It was dark as ink in the room now, and the two of them lay there without a sound, as though they hadn't even the strength left to talk. But she clutched his hand, and after a while Mi Gao said "I guess you haven't had dinner." Xu Lili let go. Mi Gao turned on the light, and Xu Lili raised her hand to shield her eyes. Mi Gao's gaze swept over her naked body, and she noticed. She moved her hand down again to protect her lower body, while calling him a low-life. Mi Gao laughed and dropped her clothes onto her. Their clothes were in various states of dishevelment.

Mi Gao took Xu Lili to the restaurant he always went to, and ordered fried mushrooms and steamed carp along with the bracken fronds and daylilies. The carp was from Shandian Lake. Mi Gao said, "Tomorrow I'll take you there." Xu Lili didn't respond, she was entwined with him from top to toe. Having not seen each other for half a year, they'd both changed. Some of it was visible, some of it wasn't. She was thinner, probably to do with her mother passing away.

"Aren't you dizzy?" Mi Gao cautiously asked. "This is the plateau, you can get short of oxygen."

Xu Lili said, "I was fine in Lhasa, and I'll never be short of oxygen around you."

Mi Gao instinctively looked around him. Xu Lili's voice was extremely loud.

Xu Lili asked, "Am I stressing you out again? Must be you who's lacking oxygen."

Just in time, the waitress brought the fried daylilies, and Mi Gao said hurriedly, "Try them. They grow wild, and they taste pretty good."

Xu Lili said, "You like wild things, don't you, that's why you've been avoiding me?"

Mi Gao didn't want to quarrel with her, especially not in public. He dutifully laughed. "You've strayed from the topic."

Xu Lili grunted. "This time don't bother trying to hide from me."

When they got back to the hotel, they tumbled back together again. Xu Lili was a lot gentler. She carefully rubbed the wounds on his shoulders and asked if they hurt. Mi Gao retorted, "What do you think?" Xu Lili said, "Who told you to hide from me for so long? You're lucky I didn't eat you." Mi Gao said, "My flesh isn't that tasty." Xu Lili asked what he had come to this place for. The image of the woman flashed past Mi Gao's mind's eye and he hesitated, then said, "Nothing." Xu Lili said, "But you didn't have to run this far away just to hide from me." Mi Gao chuckled — "So far, and yet you still hunted me down." Xu Lili poked him with a finger: "Why did you hide from me? Am I so awful?" Mi Gao said, "I wasn't hiding from you, I just wanted to be by myself in peace for a while." Xu Lili asked, "And now? Now you're bored of the taste of the wild?" Without waiting for Mi Gao's answer she said, "I don't blame you for anything you did, but you can't just run away. Don't even think about it, have you got that?" Mi Gao nodded.

Xu Lili insisted on resting her head on Mi Gao's arm. Mi Gao tried to extract his arm a few times because it got a bit numb and he couldn't sleep. Every time he made the slightest movement, Xu Lili woke. She didn't say anything; she just rested her head more heavily. Mi Gao wondered dejectedly if she would shackle him with a chain next. He didn't regret telling her the address — he still cared for her. He was glimpsing a piece of his mind that he'd never seen before: that was yet another thing he'd gained up on the plateau. Besides, he had a secret purpose for getting her here.

After they'd eaten the next day, he said he still wanted to stay in the little town for another few days. "The air is good in this town and the pace of life is slow, not like in the city, with everyone's faces wracked with anxiety. Stay and rest for a few days, take it easy." Xu Lili was blunt: "If you stay a few days I'll stay a few days, and if you stay a lifetime I'll stay a lifetime." Mi Gao stared blankly, and Xu Lili jostled him. "What? You're afraid?" Mi Gao quickly shook his head. "As long as you don't regret it." Xu Lili taunted him. "Sheesh! None of this nonsense. Surely it's you who'll regret it." Mi Gao laughed.

And then ... Mi Gao thought to himself for a while, stroking her hair. "It is a bit long, actually. A bit of a trim, who knows, it might look even nicer." "Mmm," said Xu Lili, "it is a bit long, but in this little place ..." Mi Gao said, "It could be a souvenir." Xu Lili said, sharply sensitive, "A souvenir of what?" Mi Gao said, "A souvenir of a new beginning." Xu Lili had a distant look in her eyes. Mi Gao wanted to slap himself.

Mi Gao brought Xu Lili out of the hotel, across the junction, then about a hundred meters more until they reached the mouth of the alleyway. With Xu Lili taking the lead, Mi Gao could stride right into the woman's fortress. He'd traced her for the best part of a year but hadn't encountered her at close quarters. He wasn't at all clear about what his aim was, perhaps an encounter at close quarters would let him decide how to respond to the man?

Mi Gao's heart pounded violently when they saw Fengfeng's Barber Shop. It was business hours and the door was open, but there was a curtain hanging in the doorway. The curtain was made of oval beads strung together. Without a breeze, every bead was still and quiet.

"Is this it?" asked Xu Lili.

Mi Gao nodded.

The moment Xu Lili lifted the bead curtain, Mi Gao suddenly grabbed her arm. Xu Lili looked at him in confusion. "What's up?" Mi Gao started pulling her away. Xu Lili cried out, "What are you doing?" His steps quickened, pulling her along. Mi Gao said, "Don't cut it, actually. I like you with long hair." Xu Lili muttered, "You're weird." But her whole face was beaming with delight and surprise. "If you like it I'll just leave it then. Why are we running?" Mi Gao said, "To see the birds! If we're too slow the birds will fly off."

2016

I See the Light

Ge Shuiping / 葛水平
Translated by Shelly Bryant

1

In the early spring, especially just before the planting season, someone was getting anxious at Shanshen'ao, wondering, "Why hasn't anyone called me to come out from the mountain? If they don't call me soon, I'll be too busy to go."

Li Laifa, who used to be busier than the cadres, was finally feeling lonely. He did not like to be left out in the cold, so it seemed that, even during the extremely busy spring season, his mind was still stuck in the past. The past — ah! that was a busy time! — when the big steamed white buns gradually shoved the pot cover open and spread their fragrance, like the smell of a coquettish woman at an evening meal, or the smell of peach blossoms in the mud. That feeling of hunger and thirst bursting the heart caught Li Laifa off guard, and blossoms of love once again burst forth in his memory.

The wind of the past, the moon of the past, the Shanshen'ao of the past made all the days that came after such a bore.

Li Laifa would not take it lying down. He was a man. What man wasn't on the go all his life? From morning to night, he did his best to look busy. Busy about what? Everyday things, all the little things that make up a life.

On the path out of the mountain at Shanshen'ao that spring, some people witnessed Li Laifa's feet kicking up the dust as he hit the road again.

Li Laifa hung a red cloth tassel from the front of his pants, which flapped playfully. When seen from a distance, the speck of red drawing near let people know that he was in a hurry to get out of the mountains. The red that hung at the front of his crotch was very garish, the kind of red cloth tassel that drove away evil spirits, but it was also a mark of his identity. Whenever Li Laifa was coming out of the mountains, he would shout to others, "Hey, do you need anything? I'm going to descend the mountain." Everyone in Shanshen'ao would stick their heads out of their cave dwellings to see him walking by, his neck hanging as if on a rope. If you gave him money, you got nothing in return, and the money would be gone too. What could you do if the money was gone? When you had a headache or fever, he would come, trying to treat you and pacify you. No matter whether you were getting better, this would settle his debt. As this went on, who would dare to give him any more money? So feeling the snubs of the other people, Li Laifa walked off into the distance, resentful over others' rejection of his generous offer.

Li Laifa was not resented because of his appearance. It was because of an exciting story involving him some time earlier, and until now, there were some matters that the people of Shanshen'ao just could not make head or tail of. Back then, there was something in Li Laifa's mindset which did not exist in the mindset of the other people of Shanshen'ao. What was it? It was like the craftiness of a farmer, yet it was a ridge higher than the craftiness of a farmer, and it was really very interesting.

The story dates back to Li Laifa's youth, when he lived in poverty, not only lacking sufficient food, but also without proper clothing or shelter. Li Laifa was the oldest of five siblings, and the four who came after him were all girls. The responsibility for the household would fall onto his shoulders as soon as he reached adulthood — that much he knew. In his father's sighs, he could hear that the old man did not think Li Laifa could shoulder that responsibility. At night, all five children huddled on the bed beneath a single blanket. During the day, two of his sisters took turns wearing a single pair of pants to the outhouse. When Li Laifa reached the age of eighteen, it was time for him to marry, but since he didn't have a cave dwelling, who would want to marry him? The matchmaker ran to and fro until her legs and mouth grew thin, but even then, Li Laifa could only fly in an airplane in his dreams, and still, he could not fly very high. As it happened, one day when his father was chiseling out a house in the mountain for him, cliff debris collapsed on him and he died of suffocation under a pile of rubble. There was no head of the house anymore. Li Laifa's hope of getting married and living on his own also vanished.

How shall we describe what came after that? The word "poor" lays a foundation. That Li Laifa could not bear a heavy burden had something to do with his appearance.

And what did he look like? Li Laifa had a small head. Like his father, Li Douming, there was not much flesh on his face, while his neck was as thin as twine. Two ears protruded from the fleshless bones behind his cheeks, like two coins. When he walked, one shoulder blade was raised too high and the other one tipped toward the ground, a little like a perplexed shadow under a lamp. If you went closer and looked at his back view, his skeleton looked like it was tied to a string and pulled upwards, ready to scatter at any time. Even when he wanted to project it, his voice was always thin, like a quiet falsetto. He was small, and his neck and head seemed to be joined by a tendon. Sometimes when you called him and he turned around too fast, he looked like dough about to be twisted into a pretzel before your eyes. In this way, his mother did not see him as capable of carrying a heavy burden, but in Li Laifa's mind, he felt he should shoulder the entire burden of the family.

Some things are closely linked to spring, not only because it is the germinating season, but also because it is warm, like a quilt, and full of love.

It was a spring morning. The primroses, apricot blossoms, peach blossoms, and pear blossoms were blooming one after the other. Golden bees flitted about like freely escaping pistils, leading Li Laifa on, and he walked and walked. He walked all the way to the sunken grave where his ancestors were buried. The amber morning sun cast a gilded light over the hole. Scattered wildflowers swayed, and bees flew about collecting pollen with their tiny feelers. Watching for a while, he began to feel it was odd. Why did the bees need to collect pollen? Li Laifa drew nearer, wanting to have a better, more leisurely look. Before he knew what had landed on his body, he was promptly stung on the nose. It hurt! It was so unbearable he grew quite angry, wanting to tear the wildflowers to bits. Picking up a dry piece of wood left from last winter, he ran at the honeycomb, intending to jump and stab it, but he tripped and fell, tumbling right into the grave.

The ancestors of the people of Shanshen'ao were so poor they had always relied on the mercy of heaven for their sustenance. No one there was very bold, so during their lives, they lived meagerly, and when they died, they did not even have a good grave to rest in. Just as this thought crossed Li Laifa's mind, he saw a heap of rotting coffin boards. What was strange was that a dim light radiated from them, shining into the darkness. He stooped to pick up a piece of the coffin board, not realizing that it was phosphorus that caused the glow. In his mind, this was something rare, and rare things always had a purpose. There was a gap in his thinking, but it was barely perceptible. His active mind made him close his eyes. He saw a ball of bright light just on the eyelids, and he saw a circle of a soft outline of something... then, nothing. With all his might, Li Laifa squeezed his eyes shut, feeling a fluttering sensation, as if golden stars were rushing towards him. First of all, he could be certain that this was not the mighty breath of spring. What it was was a feeling between vitality and despair, between darkness and light, between the danger of the cavedin grave and the shelter of the mud. It was the classic signs of oxygen deficiency.

This was how the clever Li Laifa came to know that the mission of bearing the family burden had fallen to him. Where could he draw strength and confidence for bearing this load? He could not fathom it for the moment. He sat on that grave, going out early and returning home late at night, sitting on it for five whole days. On the evening of the fifth day, Li Laifa suddenly saw the light, as if he were visited by a phantom.

2

On that spring night, the

peasants of Shanshen'ao who were gathered outdoors saw a ball of light flickering vaguely on the mountain on the opposite side of the valley. A few children pointed at it, shouting, "Look! It's moving!"

Then came the sound of birdsong — or at least, they heard a few birds chirping.

But nothing blocked the view of the peasants.

Some older people started to recount some ghost stories. One said, "Long ago, people who had died became ghosts, and the ghosts could float or walk in midair." His old face, wrinkled with age, drew into a grimace. The ghosts appearing in the dark made people's hair stand on end. But as the story got passed on from one generation to another among the people of Shanshen'ao, the love of the ghosts seemed to make them gentle and generous.

But the children recoiled into the crowd in fear — after all, what adults were talking about was a world of silence, and not things living in the real world. The adults would occasionally call, "Boo!" to frighten the children and women and make the hair stand straight up.

One woman said, "Can't you all talk about proper things?"

A man replied, "What things are proper after dark?"

She said, "All of you are so improper."

The men stopped talking.

The children grew restless again, asking them to finish the story. Their hearts were seized by the limitless possibilities the narration could lead to, and they pestered the adults to clarify these simple, yet perfect, stories. What gave them all a shock was Li Laifa's sudden appearance, coming from who knew where.

He said, "I had a dream in the middle of the night, and in my dream I met the Jade Emperor of Heaven. He told me that if I saw something glowing on the opposite mountain, it was the celestial book he dropped from heaven for me. See! Look at the glow on the peak opposite us. It might be the celestial book the Jade Emperor told me about."

Li Laifa bent his back like a wooden bench, begging for someone to go with him to the mountain opposite them.

His mother stood at the door of their cave dwelling and shouted, "Laifa! Laifa! Hurry home to eat porridge!"

He called back, "What porridge? I don't want porridge. I want to eat steamed buns."

"It's not the New Year, or any special festival, and Laifa wants to eat steamed buns? It would be more sensible if he wanted to eat *wotou*, but eating steamed buns is a little ridiculous," said the people standing nearby, laughing.

Li Laifa's behavior had grown a bit erratic, as if some god of his own really had possessed him. Puzzled, the people looked at him and smiled. Some started to tease him, "Laifa, no one will go with you. If you're not afraid of ghosts stalking you, go on to the mountain opposite and have a look. See if it's the Jade Emperor's celestial book."

Li Laifa replied, "Hey, be careful! The gods have a thousand eyes and a thousand hands!"

The faint, dark mountain was visible in the distance. Li Laifa's silhouette as he walked toward it was like an upright stick, jumping, hopping, and leaping into the darkness of the mountain.

The people of Shanshen'ao suddenly felt their bodies and hearts stirring. They had never given Li Laifa any thought in the past, and had never really thought of him as much of a character. He was someone you didn't have to expend too much energy analyzing. They simply waited to see his rare treasure. When he descended the slope, he was clamping a package wrapped in red cloth under his arm. He said mysteriously, "It was a book, but with no words."

No words! And yet he called it a book!

3

Spring had passed, and summer had arrived. Jokes about Li Laifa flew about, emerging from curtains of rain and following the scenery along the path out of the mountains. Huge rivers swelled outside the mountains, and the sun was shining brightly. The jokes spread and were slowly treated as reality. It was true! People from outside the village wanted to give it a try, all because there was no proper doctor in the village, making Li Laifa like a life-saver to them.

The first time he gave someone medical treatment, Li Laifa could not quite grasp what was happening. He was really just trying to find out how much the people trusted him.

He stood at the door of the cave and looked eagerly at his visitor.

The visitor said, "I've heard you can help with certain things. I've got an emergency situation, so I came to see if you can cure it."

A warm, intoxicating expression floated across Li Laifa's face. It had begun.

Saying nothing, he backed serenely into the cave, like waters receding from the beach. There was an incense burner on a long narrow table at one end of the cave. He lit three joss sticks and stood up, moving to sit on the brick bed. As he sat, his hipbone sounded like it was about to fall apart.

Li Laifa asked, "Who's sick?"

The guest said, "My daughter. She's got fever. Her head feels like she's on fire. She's dry, not sweating at all."

"What day did this start?"

"July 18."

"Take an old scallion root and dry ginger and boil them until the flavor comes out, then make her drink it. What did you bring with you when you came?"

"I was in a hurry," the visitor said. "I didn't bring anything."

Li Laifa said, "If you didn't bring anything, how can I give you the medicine to take home? Next time you come, make a few steamed buns. These aren't for me to eat, but to feed to the gods."

Saying that, he jumped down from the bed, picked up a *wotou* from the kitchen stove, tore off a small piece, and squeezed it in his hand. He blew on it and recited some phrase, then walked to the end of the cave and kneaded a bit of incense from the incense burner. Unexpectedly, he stomped his foot, causing dirt to fall from everywhere, then he finally asked the visitor to take the "medicine" home. He said, "Go back and divide it into portions to be eaten over three days. When she's chewed and swallowed it, drink the concoction of old scallion root and dry ginger, taking it all down in one gulp without stopping. You'll see improvement in three days.

Li Laifa did not say she would be well in three days. He just said they would see improvement.

When he had seen the visitor off, Li Laifa wanted to say something — some heartfelt words — but he had no idea who to say them to. The thick gloom deep inside the cave was a stark contrast to the bright sunlight outside, like the inner conflict he felt now.

Li Laifa relieved himself in the toilet opposite the cave. As he was pulling on his trousers, he looked at his old cave dwelling. The cave did not even look as nice as the toilet. The stone wall of the toilet had pumpkin flowers, hyacinth flowers, and loofa flowers blooming on it, in patches of yellow, white, and red, attracting many bees, alongside the flies, to flit among them. Li Laifa felt like crying. Salty tears gushed from his eyes, and his heart raced. He waited for someone to come. The narrow winding path on Shanshen'ao was empty, without a soul in sight.

His mother brought a bowl of porridge and placed it on the windowsill of the cave. The porridge was still steaming. His mother called, "Come and eat, Laifa."

He glared at his mother emotionally. It was like he had a wad of cotton stuffed into his mouth. He couldn't eat the porridge; he just wanted to eat steamed buns. The bowl of porridge, not being steamed buns, made Li Laifa turn red with anger. He twisted his neck, and his tongue curled up. He decided to do something that would shock the people of Shanshen'ao. Thinking of what existed now — everything — he felt it was not enough. He gave a loud laugh, and suddenly blacked out. His mother jumped and shouted, "Help! I'm afraid my Laifa is having a seizure!"

But he wasn't having a seizure. He had gone crazy.

Laifa said, "Mother, I am possessed by gods."

His mother passed this along to the people of Shanshen'ao. The gods were with him, and they needed to have a period of time to test him. The gods had possessed Laifa, and he had become confused about the real world.

Having said this, Li Laifa said no more. In his silence, he hoped to awaken the people of Shanshen'ao.

He was like prop, ready to perform on the stage of human life. He started by going into a trance, and the trance was a betrayal of his consciousness. He had a certain consciousness, and it was guided by the gods. He was experiencing the pleasure of realizing his goal in his consciousness.

He woke up from the trance a month later, seeming to be restored to his former, normal self. No one would be allowed to know the secret of Laifa's trance. In this renewed state, he moved his pair of ridiculous feet forward, and once again won the affirmation of the people of Shanshen'ao.

A personage had turned up in Shanshen'ao. Just like that, the rice-flour steamed buns in his cave dwelling increased. When the poor fell sick, they tried to put up a hard fight with the celestial king. They were no more willing to get medicine from the shop than they were able to win the fight. They would rather make some steamed buns and seek help from one possessed by spirits, so Li Laifa's business grew from a trickle to a flood, suddenly beginning to look quite prosperous. He sat cross-legged on the bed, thin as fire kindling, eyes wide open watching his visitors, and also expanding the nerves in his ears and nose. He took one of the eight steamed buns the visitor had brought and tore off a small piece. He blew a few immortal breaths on it, muttered a few barely distinguishable words, then sent it back with the visitor. The visitor, neither hearing or seeing a thing, took the piece of steamed bun the size of his own thumb and sulkily departed.

With such a simple, repetitive process, a whole pile of steamed buns grew inside Li Laifa's cave dwelling. He decided to turn the steamed buns into capital to dig three cave houses, decorating the mouth with bricks. This was the style of a wealthy man.

His mother said happily that this was good. Otherwise, the steamed buns would grow a layer of green fuzz in the heat.

4

During those years of poverty, those who helped Li Laifa dig his cave houses asked for nothing in return but a full belly. It took only a few days for one cave house to be dug. Those people who had headaches and fever sought Li Laifa out for help, and more and more people came to help with digging the cave houses because of his "skills." Taking advantage of the situation, Li Laifa decided to dig two more cave houses. The completion of three new cave houses put him in a whole different realm than the people of Shanshen'ao.

The cave houses of Li Laifa activated every cell in the people of Shanshen'ao. The 50-mile mountain road was like a long ruler, and the big steamed white buns the scales on the ruler, enticing the villagers. Everything looked bleak, and illness only made the villagers' poverty worse. When villagers saw large group of sweaty people rushing in from the hills of Shanshen'ao and their clumsy feet attacking the streets of Shanshen'ao, their inner misery cried out for the just gods to spare them some of the steamed white buns.

Li Laifa's mind had completely entered another distant land of the imagination. This was not the same humble, polite Laifa with his hanging arms and frame like a wooden bench. He had become stylized. His alienation from and unfamiliarity with the people of Shanshen'ao made his relationship with the villagers wither. But this did not bother Li Laifa.

When the new cave houses were complete, the people of Shanshen'ao did not come to warm them with their presence, but the autumn flies did. These autumn flies buzzed and bustled about in the air, leading Li Laifa out of one cave, then into the next. His happiness was as bright as the sun squeezing in through the wooden lattice over the windows. The autumn flies danced in the dazzling light and shadows as if drunk. From time to time, Li Laifa's tongue flicked out from the corner of his mouth, as if licking an invisible piece of candy inside, stirring up his gastric juices. He even grabbed one fly aggressively and wrapped it in a piece of steamed bun the size of his thumb, then told one visitor to take the whole thing home as a healing concoction.

Life's stage is like a play, watching the sun rise, make its westward journey, then set. Night fell from the top of the high cave, falling so hopelessly. It was all right during the day, but at night? Nighttime made Li Laifa feel alone, with the moon casting cloudy shadows and the birds resting on their branches. The night also made Li Laifa feel stirred and agitated. When he couldn't sleep, he went out of his cave and looked at the village spread out before him. The wind was chilling him to the bone and freezing his joints, and Shanshen'ao was as dark as the bottom of a wok. One year after another rushed by so quickly. Surely he could not live his days out in the cold! On the bed of other people's caves were vague swaying figures, and their breathing, whether shallow or heavy, evoked feelings of roaring desolation in his mind and his ear canal, which then ran down his spine. The people of Shanshen'ao had stirred up the night into something vast and bloated, with a penetrating breeze. At the end of the day, Li Laifa was a grown man, and the darkness in every corner was attacking his lean frame.

He wanted a woman.

Li Laifa took a fancy to the wife of a man named Wang Laixin, from Bugou. She happened to fall ill at just this time.

One of the clouds under the spring moon drifted west and the other east, quietly converging on Shanshen'ao. Bent over in his effort to climb the mountain, Wang Laixin came to see Li Laifa for medical help. Li Laifa insisted that his wife come to Shanshen'ao to see him, saying that only then could the evil air in her body be removed more quickly. Wang Laixin brought his wife over, transporting her down from a little hilltop on a donkey, opening a story of romance in Shanshen'ao.

Wang Laixin's wife was actually suffering from mental hysteria brought on by extreme poverty. With steamed white buns to eat and a warm place to sleep, she was well within half a month from the time she arrived in Shanshen'ao. She wanted to leave, but Li Laifa would not allow it. From the bed by the cave, she could only look at the notch in the mountains in the distance, where two children were playing in the mud. She did not know why, but one of the little guys started crying, and with one chasing the other, they returned to their cave, startling a group of sparrows, which in turn disturbed the peach blossoms on a tree until the petals fell off. The woman sighed slightly, and her breath was like a breeze blowing off the dust from the petals. It was so soft it could leap.

Li Laifa drew near and daintily pulled a strand of hair from her ear between his middle finger and thumb, extending his other digits in fine fashion, like an opera singer. The strand of hair brushed her cheek. He blew on the hair. It itched and she bit her lower lip, straining to keep herself from laughing out loud. Just then, Li Laifa held up the bucket of steamed white buns and, looking at Li Laixin's wife, he too felt like laughing — laughing at her hair as it twisted itself in knots in the mischievous wind, then disentangled, following the fits of her laughter.

A person cannot control the wind, so she might as well give in and sway according to it. Her face became fuzzy in the wind. Nothing but the wind understands amorous feelings. A feeling of apprehension suddenly seized Li Laifa. This woman was laughing, but her laughter was not coquettish enough.

Li Laifa raised the steamed white bun in his hand and said, "It smells good, doesn't it?"

Suppressing her smile, she nodded.

He said, "It has been fed

to you so you would become as white and fleshy as a silkworm."

Wang Laixin's wife wanted to snatch the steamed bun from Li Laifa, but she pulled her hand back.

Li Laifa said, "I want to sleep with you tonight, navel to navel."

Not waiting for an answer from Wang Laixin's wife, he stood on tiptoes and leant toward her face to kiss her. Lowering his body, he hugged her thigh, and then suddenly straightened up like a carp jumping out of water before pressing himself right against her.

This time, the woman's coquettish laughter was so loud it filled the cave.

A month later, Wang Laixin finally returned to take his wife home.

The spring breeze blew softly. Through the open windows, he could see the earthworm-like mountain path and the donkey and the woman it carried swaying as they walked into the distance. Eventually, they were buried in deep sunlight, lost in the chiaroscuro of the other side of the mountain, and finally vanishing like a dream.

The dreamer awoke, feeling small and lonely. Li Laifa grumbled, "Farther, farther, farther." Then he started crying.

Having gotten used to tasting sweetness, Li Laifa felt he needed a new crop to replace the old. The clouds that had passed over the mountain, the rain that had splashed on the mud, a dream that had passed in the long night could not disappear just like that.

After that, he thought of ways to cajole those women who needed his treatment to come see him in person. Graceful and charming women adorned Shanshen'ao's dusty road like blooming flowers. Li Laifa settled each woman who came into the mountains onto the bed in turn, drinking brown sugar water and eating steamed white buns. The women's faces reflected their satisfaction. They had enough to eat and drink. As they stared greedily at the steamed buns in the wooden bucket, they asked, "Li Laifa, is there anything you lack?"

And he would say, "I don't

have you."

The women asked, "I guess you have enough steamed buns?"

They would then take two steamed buns in their little cloth bags to take home to their children.

The people in Shanshen'ao held big bowls in their hands. When it was warm, they sat in the shade under a tree, and when it was cold, they ate in the sun, squatting in groups here and there, forming an open-air eating field. They gathered here not just for a spacious place to eat, but for entertainment provided by Li Laifa. The mouths of the men left the lips of the bowls and their eyes sought out Laifa in his cave. The wives of these men stood in the doorway with a brush, waiting to wash the pots, shouting for their men to come back to the caves. They became anxious as their men were too busy to heed their call, and soon these men would see brushes flying in their directions.

At that moment, Li Laifa's mother saw an evil air come from her son. The women who came to seek medical help from him had neglected the gift of steamed white buns. When his mother discovered how serious this problem was, there was not a single steamed bun left. She devised many plans for exacting her revenge, the first being to stand in front of the door to keep any women out.

Li Laifa said, "Good for you if you can even keep me out."

In the days after that, his mother put soda in the brown sugar water and smiled as she offered it to the women to drink. The bitter water not only went through the intestines to the belly, but also raced along the neck to the head. No longer seeking treatment, the women did not allow Li Laifa to touch them — not even with his fingertips.

For a long time, the sky above Shanshen'ao echoed with a woman's shouted curses. Those women who had before returned repeatedly simply vanished into thin air.

5

It was a peaceful season. Spring was gone, and autumn would come. Li Laifa liked to repeat a phrase often spoken by storytellers: "It is indeed a rare arrow for which, when the soft silk string is pulled, the penetrating shot is sure."

Li Laifa was that silk-stringed bent bow, ready to go.

He waited patiently and tearfully, and the entertainment in Shanshen'ao provided by Li Laifa quietened down amid the loneliness. Thanks to his dalliance with the women, that was the last thing the villagers inevitably remembered with fondness when they thought about the celestial book. Whether it was a wordless book or not, Li Laifa could no longer remain cool. Li Laifa would wait no more. He went out of the mountains himself instead. Unfortunately, despite the steps he took, nothing could deliver him from his desolation.

Li Laifa fell victim to an epidemic when he was forty, and his high fever would not abate. He was confined to his cave for three days. He looked at the shimmering flame of the oil lamp, then stared at the layer of mud on the cave wall. Markings of different shapes and colors could be seen clearly on the mud wall. Flying insects as small as a single grain of rice danced in circles before the lamp, flitting about or stopping. In the midst of empty loneliness and an unwillingness to be resigned to his fate, days past were reflected on the mud walls little by little. Surging water and the evening glow, rain, snow, wind, clouds, rustling grass blades, and the chirruping insects — endless natural phenomena of a season are buried in the chaotic world of human affairs, filled with sorrow and joy. Li Laifa felt life now was not the same as before. It was as if the days had multiplied, and the extra days had begun to disintegrate his mind. He gradually grew disappointed with himself. Some things had moved far away, flickering in the distance then showing up again, revealed and hidden in alternation. Inexplicably, he hated his mother. Thinking of those women hidden in that unforgettable time and place, he mustered his final strength to laugh once more.

Three days later, he was left with just skin and bones. Using his last ounce of strength, Laifa burned the celestial book on the flame of the oil lamp. Where the smoke scattered, the mist and fog around the peak of Shanshen'ao condensed into an inky cloud. He looked at the cluster of inky clouds, then let his eyes droop, expiring in peace.

Because the deceased Li Laifa did not have a woman, a brick with a woman's name engraved on it was placed in the coffin. The woman's name was Zhuan Hong, meaning "to turn red" or "prosperous." That day, Zhuan Hong and Laifa closed their eyes together, and she was wrapped in red cloth and placed on the pillow beside him.

According to the customs passed down in Shanshen'ao, when an unmarried man passed away, a brick wrapped in red cloth was placed in the coffin with him. This was called "inviting the brick." The brick named Zhuan Hong was very happy, for once she fell asleep, she would not wake again.

2008

Prose

Clamour

Siren / 塞　壬
Translated by Florence Woo

Not even in my dreams would those noises dissipate, even though I have shut the windows and drawn the curtains tight. I am recoiling, shrinking. Chaotic and heinous like flying blades, the noises are tracking me by my scent, hunting me, hounding me into my dreams. I see myself under their glint: a careworn face, distraught features, a frantic figure, sorrow emanating from the depths of my eyes. Indeed, I am always retreating, running away — an itinerant between Guangzhou, Shenzhen, and Dongguan, I have been drifting and drifting in the midst of this colossal clamour. It is dense, and as oppressive as loneliness. I cannot escape. It surrounds me continuously.

I have tried to scream at the top of my lungs; I have kicked and stomped, in an effort to tear apart this terrifying, impenetrable clamour. But it is impregnable. Rather, it flings each of my screams back at me, with incontestably violent strength. And then, I am submerged, and no one can hear what I was screaming about. After that, I gradually become mute, with my lips sealed, my gaze lowered, having become accustomed to the murkiness.

Some sounds are palpable, like solid matter covered in sharp spikes. Some sounds are incorporeal, but have a force field around them — as soon as I try to say the words "pierce" or "crush" , my body reflexively responds with an "ouch!" . I yowl in spite of myself.

And then the pain arrives. I wake up in my bed shrieking. I have heard my anguished and desperate cries in my sleep. That scene has played in my dreams again. Vividly, repetitively, it torments me —

A motorcycle comes up from behind me, soundlessly — The rear passenger reaches out to snatch my shoulder-bag — I am pushed to the ground, but still clinging on to my bag — The bike speeds on, dragging me behind it, for a few dozen metres — There is blood and bones and searing pain and screaming ... and after that, grief-filled sobbing.

During the day, I am so preoccupied with making ends

meet that I can push that out of my mind. However, like clockwork this would invariably appear in my dreams, wounding me again and again. That cry is fated to echo ceaselessly throughout my future, echoing relentlessly and throwing light onto what the rest of my life will look like: depressed, anxious, despondent, reeking of turmoil. I am very sensitive to the noise of motorcycles. Whenever an engine revs up, followed by roars one louder than the last — vroom Vroom VROOM! — anxiety, tension, and an inexplicable dread would seize me, and in that instance I would again hear my own anguished cry coming from the depths of my life. It seems as if a great eagle is casting the shadow of its wings onto the ground, and the hunt is about to begin; meanwhile, the fate of the hunted is unmistakably plain.

This hideous scene frequently plays before my mind's eye like a movie. This malaise in my heart, this inexorable nightmare, is enough for me to lose my mind. "Robbery" — a word filled with violence and gore — happened five times in my wandering life in the South. Surely I cannot write it off as a coincidence; I have come to believe that it is tied to my fate. The roar of the motorcycle and my cries have joined together in my mind into a shrill clamour. Under its limelight, my life is laid bare for all to see, and so is my fragile body, collapsed into a small heap on the ground. That clamour ravages me repeatedly even long after the incident, and I can only choose to mourn silently.

All the girls in the office have experienced robbery, and some have experienced worse. Sometimes they would show off where on their bodies they were hurt. Their expression is one of entertainment and merriment, as they compare who had a more terrifying robbery experience than whom. That such a bloody scene could be described so cheerfully and used as small talk material! I think many of us have been desensitised by the ubiquity of such experiences. Indeed, we have all been desensitized by life itself.

One of the girls said, "When

they snatched my bag, I just let go right away and let them take it. When they pushed me to the ground, I climbed back up, chop-chop, just like that ..." I mulled over that phrase: "chop-chop" . As killed and seasoned way to deal with it, to be sure, so polished that it smacked of being self-congratulatory. And yet how heart-breaking is it when you think more deeply about it! I can never seem to talk about it as casually as others can. It is not necessarily because my experience and injuries were more painful than other people's — it's just that I can't ever learn to disregard it. I don't know if the same scenes also appear in their dreams, or if, as in my case, they would develop gradually into a sickness of the heart, coagulating into a tumour. Time does not cure all this. Ah, if only I could learn to forget!

Back in the winter of 2001, I was living in Shipai Village in Guangzhou. The alleys there were dark and damp, crammed with buildings where lived all sorts of people: labourers, hawkers, students, migrant workers, prostitutes, criminals, con artists, drug addicts, hooligans. When such a motley crew are packed together in such a small area, the word "grime" immediately comes to mind. But they also emitted an alluring atmosphere of disorder, danger, and unrest — as well as a grimy sort of vitality.

There was a long corridor in the building where I was renting, with rental units on either side, some twenty of them, housing such people of dubious origins. To my left lived a young local Guangdong couple with a child. No one knew what they did for a living. The man was short, brawny, and swarthy. When he had his trouser legs rolled up, one could see that his calves were round and solid. The woman had a sallow face and dishevelled hair, and her gaze was always lowered. She would walk around pitter-patter inside the flat, in a pair of plastic slippers. They seemed to be living in a shadow. Then again, their whole lives appeared sunless. I never heard them singing or humming; they even seldom smiled.

To my right lived three

seductive women. They would always go out late at night, wearing dark eyeshadow. Scantily clad and cigarettes between their lips, they would stagger home drunkenly in the small hours. They were always on their cell phones and were always giggling. I did not care to guess their occupation. Across from me lived a few young men. As soon as they got home they would swing the door wide open, then start to talk loudly and crank up the music. There would be the clanging of wash basins. The boys would keep going in and out of the flat, and you could hear them crooning a tune as they went about.

During the day I worked at an advertising company, and every evening I dragged my weary self home. Sleep was my only pleasure in life. To fall asleep is to fall into sweet dreams and hopes, into love and adventure, into springtime and childhood. There was no better cure for irritation, fear, and anxiety than to lock the world outside and return to the boundless tranquillity of the soul. What better way to rest thoroughly, to let tranquillity flood the mind, than to relinquish the body to clean bed sheets and comfort?

Inevitably I would be woken up by the noise of rapid kicking at the door. It must be a pair of sturdy boots. The noise, besides being harsh and savage, brandished menace: *Open the door, and on the double*. This perverse interlude was intensely intrusive. It made you panic, and made your heart race wildly, drumming like mad. Even I — the peaceful and law-abiding citizen that I am — would feel like I had done something criminal and was now found out, and that they were here to arrest me. Whenever I heard this door-kicking noise, my first irrational instinct would be to hide. They're here to check temporary residency permits. Shipai Village was a den of iniquity — just next doors lived three women of the night — and the local patrol would often come in the middle of the night to check the residents' permits.

There was a large ruckus outside the door, and all the tenants were woken up. All those who did not have permits had to be registered. Some others were taken away, while others were arguing, swearing, begging, berating — it was veritable mayhem. I poked my head out of the door and timidly passed my permit through the crack in the door for them to see. I was resisting. I would not allow them into my home. One of them flashed his torch inside, and I shuffled over to block the light. I could not calm down for a long time even after they were done. I was shaking as if I had been shocked, and the wild pounding in my chest was still going on. My mind was still full of that dreadful kicking sound — Thud, thud, thud! Thud, thud, thud! I hugged myself and tried to settle myself down. But all I could hear was thud, thud, thud! Thud, thud, thud! Thud, thud, thud ...

The young couple were just on the other side of the wall. The head of my bed was likely right against theirs, as I often get woken up by a clonking noise from behind my head. It was them making love, going at it so violently that their wooden four-poster was quaking and knocking rhythmically against the wall. I woke up. There were clear sounds of wild panting and soft moaning. Then they ramped it up more, and the rapid clonking began pounding into my heart, blow by blow. I felt the wall shake. The floor began trembling along with it. I felt a chill along my back, and my throat was parched. I wanted some water. But I could only lie there, not daring to move. I even heard their bed collapse — he gave out a loud roar, and she whimpered weakly over and over. I tried as hard as possible not to imagine what was going through their minds when they made those noises. However, as much as I forbade myself from imagining, I suffered from the torment of imagination. Their noises were attacking me. Their wanton indulgence was attacking me. The noises were disturbing me, a quiet person. They were hurting me. They made me aware that I was lonely and forsaken, lost and friendless, exiled to a dark corner to languish and fend for myself. For me, those nights were steeped in agony.

I know, to a couple living in poverty, sex was a most

sumptuous feast; that burly Guangdong man and his wife were just seeking to escape all their difficulties in life, through pursuing carnal pleasures with abandon. Clonk-clonk-clonk, clonk-clonk-clonk, that noise knocked on the wall over and over again, striking at one who was lonely and disconsolate. And thus it would go, through the dark night until daybreak.

And their child would always begin screeching at five in the morning. It was a penetrating sound, ferocious, intractable, as if the boy was spending all his might to create such a noise. Each cry was punctuated with a sob and a gasp, as if he was fighting for his life. That noise felt like it was stained with blood and giving off an odour of anguish. That was a very distressing noise, guaranteed to lead to insanity over time.

There was something tremendously stinging in this wailing, like a splinter piercing into one's heart, hinting vaguely of impending doom. Even though the couple would stop him, it was quite irritating to be woken up at five in the morning. It would affect my mood that day; the wounded cry would hover over me for the rest of the day. I might forget my keys or my phone, or even what I had planned to do at work, and be miserable. Once I saw the boy. He was standing there unsteadily, holding onto the door frame. He was maybe three years old, wan and frail, with skinny arms and legs, and tiny shoes on his feet. I walked up to him, and he lifted his head to look at me. He had gleaming dark eyes and almost no eyebrows. He parted his lips slightly as if wanting to smile, but before he could form one, his lips closed shut again. He was such a young child, and yet his expression was one of loneliness and melancholy, as if he had already understood many things of this world. How could he have such energy to produce such sharp cries, cries that felt like his life was on the line? I became afraid. I was afraid of a word, a word that I could not say out loud.

I could pretty much ignore some of the louder noises. On Sundays, the boys across the corridor would keep the front door open and blast their music. There was robustness to the music, a vigour in the upbeat tunes. Although I preferred quietude, I could find my peace and read or nap. Over time I just got used to it. If I focused on my inner mind, I wouldn't even hear the music. Yes, they were as if non-existent to me. The three sultry ladies next doors would also make all kinds of noises after midnight — swearing, quarrelling, throwing things — but these noises didn't bother me at all. They didn't have a way to worm into my heart. Later, I moved to another place, and there was construction going on, all through the night and into the early morning. The bulldozers were roaring, like thunders exploding over my head. The percussive blows of the pile-driving sounded like they were closing in on me, but I could still treat them as a part of the soundscape. I let it be part of my world, the backdrop to the night, as if they had always been there. I slept easily and soundly through all that. And even when people were renovating next doors, and the noises of hammering and drilling were boring through my skull, I found them tolerable even though they were annoying. Those were just noises of a purely physical nature, not injurious on their own.

But there is another kind of noise, one of a lower decibel level, that nonetheless creates a crushing, disconcerting, suffocating atmosphere. Just like the clamour of violence, it throws a light on my lot in life, making me see myself once again — frail, skittish, apprehensive; I see myself struggling, compromising, and falling silent in my daily existence; I see myself casting my glance down, not allowing myself to make any sound. Slowly, but surely, I become a deaf-mute, a giant vessel who swallows up all of life's fortunes, the good as well as the bad.

To this day I cannot remember what the boss of that company looked like. His facial features existed only as an abstract impression. Or perhaps I should say, I have never once looked at his face carefully. His voice seemed to emanate from his chest; it was low, abrupt, callous, like something was caught in his throat and preventing him from speaking clearly. But the tone of his voice was undeniably filled with arrogance and crassness. Everyone in the company feared that voice, a voice that veiled the space like a pervasive shadow, casting terror on everyone. I would hazard that many are still tormented by that voice even after they have left the company —

"Don't interrupt me when I'm talking ..."

"I won't have any excuses ..."

"You are all thieves, conning paycheques out of me. Thieves, all of you ..."

"Get the hell out of here ..."

No one quite knew how to act around him. The boss was dissatisfied with everything. He was always criticizing, demanding, exasperated. The secretary, a young woman called Xiaoyan, was subject to his dressing-down every day. As soon as she got a phone call from the boss, she would tremble in fear for the rest of the day. She said that the boss's voice terrified her, and she was going insane. Every time she emerged from his office, she would have been scolded invariably for things like:

— The boss suddenly saw that the newspaper that was just delivered to him looked like it had been read, because it seemed to have been unfolded. No one else was to read his newspaper ...

Or — he had already said he didn't want *pu'er* tea for now; why did she make him *pu'er* again ...

Or — he had changed the time for the meeting, why didn't she inform the staff ...

It was all sorts of minutiae, all sorts of triviality: and no matter what it was, she was not allowed to explain or defend herself. All she could do was to endure the cascade of humiliation and criticism flung at her. It was not difficult to understand why — when that low, abrupt, and callous voice slapped you on the face with stinging humiliation, you are robbed of your human dignity. Simply recalling this voice was enough to make me shiver and feel a dark chill rushing over me. How cruel is this stage that we are players in, where someone always has something on you!

At first I did not really understand the poor girl when she said "I am going insane." One afternoon, I went over to the boss's office to deliver a document. I would never bring things to him when he was here, as I did not wish to face such a person. I didn't want to see him or to have him suddenly find fault with me and blast me on the spot. His office was huge, coldly but lavishly decorated. There were two thick pillars on either side, and a steep staircase leading down to the main hall of the office. The space was like an underground palace. The high ceiling made the sofas and cabinets appear tiny. The desk also appeared tiny, and as you walked in you would see a tiny person sitting at the desk. The atmosphere there was stifling, and every tiniest sound or movement was noticeable. I would soften and even out my breathing, and try to still my thumping heart.

I had thought he wouldn't be in that day, and I hadn't seen anyone in the main hall either. But then I heard voices coming from an adjacent room. "Aaah!" — I heard that man emanate a different tone now, the man who usually emitted that low, abrupt, and callous voice — "My Xiaoyan, you drive me crazy about you, my little darling, my little sweetheart ..." It was such a flippant, lecherous voice; a casual, nasal twang, it was impatient, ugly, reprobate, and thoroughly shameless ... It was nauseating. A "boom" went off in my head, and I froze there, stunned. I heard the girl pleading and sobbing in a low voice, backing away, evading him. Could she really escape, though? This was the commonest of all everyday realities in the working world. It was clear to me why she kept being scolded for no reason. Being vulnerable and inconsequential, she could change nothing whether she resisted or went with it. That sheer abuse of power and that menacing voice must torment her even in her dreams.

Over the years, I have experienced working in numerous private enterprises in the South. The most significant feature common to them all is that in each company, the whole organisation is ruled by one person — the one with the loudest voice, the only one allowed to voice, and the one whose voice dictates the fate of everyone else. The voice of this person creates an environment of stress. It creates clamour inside our minds, assaulting our bodies and our souls. And too many people have gradually become desensitised to the pain. They have lost their sorrow and their anger, and become accustomed to the darkness. And yet others are only keeping enduring silence, hiding their sorrows in the depths of their hearts, like me. How I wish I were truly deaf and mute! How I wish to communicate with those who are loveable only with my eyes, by offering them the purest smile there is in the world.

Once, a colleague and I went to attend a meeting in a large hotel, a majestic edifice by the hillside. As we got out of the car, we saw before us a great long staircase leading to the main entrance. There were no trees along the staircase, only blocks of stone and security personnel. When we entered the lobby, all we felt was an engulfing, suffocating gravity. My colleague said, "It's too quiet here. It's so quiet it's uncanny." I looked around me, and indeed, nothing was stirring, as if all sounds were sucked away, leaving nary a trace. Such silence felt ominous and disconcerting, as if something serious was about to happen. My colleague told me she was a bit scared. I asked her what she was scared about, and she replied she didn't know — she was just feeling scared.

We are so used to commotion, to chaos, to a clamorous world, that when we are suddenly dropped into a place devoid of noise, we become aware of the drumming of our own hearts. The throbbing of our heartbeats and the sound of our breathing, magnified, make us feel another kind of mighty clamour. And thus we become afraid.

But those noises will keep coming into my dreams. They are tracking me, tracking me by my scent. Once again I am illuminated by the noises, and I see my own expression: sheer terror, and the sorrow in the depths of my eyes. I hear myself screaming. And then I wake up in my bed screaming, crying, drenched in sweat. And then comes an instant of tranquillity. The world, it seems, has just woken up too, fresh and immaculate. This is the only time I can relax my body, stretch out and enjoy this momentary comfort, like a flower that blossoms for a fleeting moment out of all sight. I need this time. I press my hands against my throbbing chest and tell myself clearly: I am unscathed. I am fine. This is something I must acknowledge to myself when I am feeling calm. And then I will get out of bed, and get dressed, and then catch the bus to work.

2009

徐泽诗九首
Nine Poems by Xu Ze

Translated by Simon Patton

Xu Ze / 徐　泽

把一双干净的手伸进水里

一双婴儿的手多么干净
在劳动中流汗的手

多么干净　多么芬芳
我不喜欢涂满香粉的手

和那抓住欲望把命运交给上帝的手
在生活中许多人把手伸向金钱
或且伸进开花的裙子
探寻风的秘密
就是没有人把手伸向天空
或伸向冰凉清澈的水里
让小鱼儿吮吸手指
让河面上的青草
包裹一下内心
有人空有一双手

到离开这个世界时
还没清洗干净

Clean Hands in Water

They're so clean, babies' hands,
and so are the hands of hard workers dripping with sweat —
clean and sweet-smelling.
I don't care much for hands smeared with scented powder
or for those that grip Desire tightly
while entrusting their fate to God.
Many in this life reach out their hands to money
or to skirts bursting into flower,
hoping to uncover the wind's secrets,
but no one reaches out to the sky
or into ice-cold, transparent water
so that tiny fish can suck on their fingers
or the green weed floating on the surface of a river
can wrap for a moment their inner worlds.
For some, the possession of a pair of hands has all been in vain:
when the time comes to leave this Earth,
they haven't been washed clean

睡　眠

为了活下去
我必须按时把自己放倒在床上
睡眠对于我是度过黑夜最好的方法
我一头枕着沙丘
一头枕着雷电　雨水和风雪都在窗外
此时我和世界　都一同睡着

Sleep

In order to go on living,
I must put myself to bed at the proper time.
Sleep — for me — is the best way to get across the night.
I pillow my head on dunes of sand,
on thunder and lightning. Outside,
there is rain and wind-swept snow.
At this moment, the whole world sleeps together with

我的心灵和肉体
不会再像白天那样骚动不安

上帝真好
让我还能在一张床上平安地睡去
我不必装着烦人的傻笑
也不必痛苦和忧伤
平安地睡着　就是一种幸福
回到原始的天空的摇篮
我在梦中躲避着追捕

和一头奔跑的豪猪擦肩而过
死亡是我永久的快乐
我终有一天会放弃睡眠
两眼盯着世界和上苍
紧握的拳头也会慢慢松开……

me.
My soul doesn’t feel the constant agitation
it does during the day, nor does my flesh.

God is good: He even
grants me this peaceful sleep in a bed.
I don’t have to smile stupidly in that irritating way.
And I don’t have to feel pain or distress.
To sleep peacefully is a kind of happiness,
a return to the cradle of the primeval sky.
In my dreams I hide from whatever it is that’s hunting
me,
and a porcupine brushes past at full pelt.
Death is an everlasting joy to me.
One day, I will finally abandon sleep
and, with eyes fixed on the world
and on Heaven above, my tight fists
will slowly begin to unclench ...

母亲的身影

三十年前外婆的身影挂在墙上
三十年后母亲你的身影也挂在
墙上
作为劳动者的你们
只有在照片里才显得斯文庄重

那一双眼睛看着我
让我不敢停下脚步
母亲说　路走着
总会有出头的时候
生命的阳光为什么
总是在快绝望的时候才会出现

My Mother’s Likeness

Thirty years ago, my grandmother’s likeness was
hung up on the wall.
Now, thirty years later, yours hangs there too, Mother.
Manual workers, the pair of you,
neither of you ever looked so refined or solemn
till you had your pictures taken.
Those eyes follow my every move
so that I don’t dare stop what I’m doing.
Mother says: *As long as you keep on going,*
you’ll walk free of misery one day.
Why is it that Life’s sunshine only appears
when you find yourself on the verge of despair?

母亲　你是站着还是坐着
怎么不说一句话
这些和油灯农具
一样挂在墙上的老照片
和天空中的炊烟一样旧了
只有流水
还在叙说着心中的往事
我不敢走近家园
我怕梦的翅膀会被乡情的雨水淋湿
母亲　当我也有了第一根白发的时候
我才知什么是爱
我多么想你从照片上
走下来　再打我一下　我不会忘记你
因为你在我心中
已变成一盏温暖的灯
和岁月一起流淌　你是我灵魂中的血
直到生命的钟摆停止运动
直到风和尘埃消失

And you Mother, are you standing or sitting?
Why don't you say anything?
These faded photographs hanging on the walls
along with the oil-lamps and farm tools
are now as old as the cooking smoke hanging in the air.
Only the running water
continues to speak of those memories I carry inside me.
I don't have the courage to go anywhere near my childhood home,
afraid that the rain of my nostalgia will dampen the wings of dream.
Mother, I will know what love is
when I get my first grey hairs.
If only you could step down
out of the photograph and smack me as you used to:
I can't forget you,
because you are now warm lamp-light
in my heart, and because you are the blood of my soul,
flowing with the months and the years
until Life's pendulum stands still
and the wind and the dust vanish.

故乡的春水又涨起来了

故乡的春水又涨起来了
我用淘米的竹篮也能网到几条小鱼
那些米粒大的小鱼在墨水瓶子里游着
多么欢快　原来快乐是没有大小的
来年鱼大了　一定住在我家的水缸里

Spring Floodwaters are on the Rise Again

Spring floodwaters are on the rise in my home village again.
With the bamboo basket I use to wash rice in
I can also net a few small fish.
Small as rice-grains, these tiny fish
swim back and forth in an old ink-bottle.
They're so full of life — when it comes to happiness
it isn't a matter of big or small.
Over the coming year,
the fish'll grow bigger and no doubt they'll be moved

从屋檐瓦沟流下的水
就是世上最迷人的音乐
我还抓了许多萤火虫
照亮它水里的生活
我故乡的屋门前
就有一条宽阔的大河
有高大的老杨树和低矮的稻草堆
每当故乡的春水涨起来了
我就想回故乡　在老屋里睡一夜
把身子舒展地放平
在蚕豆花开的时候
一些梦虽是苦涩的
但总能温暖一颗贫穷的心
春水又涨起来了
那些撑着油布伞的女子
那些和往事一起游动的小鱼
那些故乡米粒一样大小的星星
又在哪里闪光呢？

to the big water-storage jar at home.
The water that flows down from the tile gutters
is the most entrancing music in the world.
I went and caught a whole lot of fireflies too
just to light up the watery lives of thosc fish.
Directly opposite the front door of my childhood home,
there's a wide river,
towering old poplar trees and low piles of rice-straw.
Whenever the Spring floods happen in my home village,
I long to go back there and sleep one night in the old house,
stretching out to my full length and lying down flat.
And when the broad beans are in flower,
certain dreams can make an impoverished heart warm,
even agonizing ones.
The Spring floods are here again,
but where are *they* now:
the women with their oil-cloth umbrellas,
the small fish swimming along with the past, and the stars
of my home village tiny as rice-grains, all shining?

小猫钓鱼

小猫钓鱼　钓给青草和红蜻蜓看
钓给太阳公公看　小猫可有耐心呢
钓了一天都没钓到一条小鱼
太阳落山了　老猫回家了
小猫不想回家　它住在稻草堆里
梦中他钓到一条大鱼
鱼把它拉到水里去了

Kitten Goes Fishing

Kitten goes fishing, fishing where the green grass
and red dragonflies can watch him —
and Grandpa Sunshine, too. What a lot of patience this
　　little cat's got!
After a whole long day, he doesn't catch a thing,
not even one tiny fish.
The sun dips behind the hills and Old Cat heads for home,
but Kitten doesn't want to leave just yet:
he makes a home for himself in a heap of rice-straw,
and dreams he has caught an enormous fish.
But the big fish pulls him into the water,

小猫的周围都是小鱼
小鱼咬着小猫的脚趾头
还戏弄小猫的胡子
痒痒　小猫醒了
那么多小鱼都到哪里去了
河水干了　天上的星星真多

where small fry surround him on all sides. They nibble his toes
and fiddle with his whiskers,
tickling him. Kitten wakes up with a start.
Now, where have all those little fishies got to?
The river is dry, but everywhere in the sky now: stars.

请允许我爱一个平凡的女人

Let Me Love an Ordinary Woman

小时候　见一个女人
总是先看她的裙子
然后是高处风景

长大后我会
看到黑暗中的泥土
泥土中温暖一生的太阳

现在　我想爱一个平凡的女人
清晨　坐车去一个工厂或者大卖场
上班　晚上带回月光水果
和刚刚出炉乳房一样金黄的面包

天冷了　肉体相互取暖
一条腿　放在另一条腿上
手足相依　平凡是多么美好

When I was a little boy, whenever I saw a woman,
first I stared at her skirt,
and then I admired the scenery of her peaks.

Later, when I was older,
I saw a soft soil in the dark,
and in that soil a sun that could keep you warm your whole lifetime.

Now, all I want is to love an ordinary woman.
and to catch the bus in the morning
to a job in a factory or a marketplace
and, when I've finished work, to bring the moon home with me,
as well as some fruit, and golden bread fresh from the oven
soft as breasts.

And when the weather turns cold, we can keep each other warm,
thigh pressed against thigh, hands
and feet intertwined —
what a beautiful thing it is to be ordinary!

这个世界真的很平常
一滴水和另一滴水穿过身体
一年四季　多少宁静的心走过一生

Our world is perfectly commonplace:
one drop of water passes through the body,
followed by another, and so many serene hearts —
Summer, Autumn, Winter, Spring —
make their way through the years.

蝴蝶来过

我五十岁开始学好
不再拈花惹草
蝴蝶来过
一般都在梦中
身体飞翔
在一如液体的花丛
吐露芬芳　一路的阳光
打在前额　如我黑暗中探寻的眼睛

把葡萄藤弯曲成思想

把轻了又轻的灵魂
打包寄往地狱
我不再想幸福这两个久违的汉字

蝴蝶来过也就来过了
一想到春天　我的身体
比冬天还要沉重

When Butterflies Come My Way

At the age of fifty I began to wise up
and I stopped fooling around with women.
If any butterfly came my way,
it was usually in dreams: bodies gliding

in liquid-like clusters of flowers,
releasing their scent. A whole road of sunshine
beat down on my forehead in the same way
my eyes scanned the dark,
twisting grape-vines into thought
and packaging up the soul,
as it got lighter and lighter
and sending it off to Hell.
I no longer think of the Chinese word for “happiness” —
a word I haven’t met with in ages.
If a butterfly comes my way, I just let it come,
but the mere thought of Spring
is enough to weigh the whole of me down
with greater weight than Winter’s.

三　月

三月　是雨水的季节
我想开膛破肚
把自己冲刷干净

March

March is the season of rain.
I’d like to split myself open
and rinse myself clean,

包括灵魂　包括假牙
包括六指琴弦上的尘埃
和旧币上风干的往事

soul and all, artificial teeth included,
and the dust on a zither,
and the past on old banknotes,
dried up by the wind.

我偶一低头
看到灯火深处
挂在珠帘上的泪滴
和不知那年那月
写给春天的诗

I happened to look down
and saw in the depths of the lamp-light
tears that clung to a crystal-bead curtain
and a poem written for the Spring
who knows when.

这辈子站在风中
却无法再回到
稻草人的故乡

I have stood out in the wind my entire life,
but can never go back to that place
scarecrows call home.

写一些雨

Writing Some Rains

雨水在天上下
雨水在地下流

Rain is falling from the sky.
Rain is running underground.

皇帝出行也下
百姓睡觉也下

When the Emperor sets out on a journey, it falls.
And when ordinary people fall asleep.

点灯时也下
黑暗时也下

At the lighting of the lamps, it falls.
And when the dark falls.

云中雨水没有脚
从山上走到河流

Inside clouds, the rain has no legs
yet it walks from the mountaintops down into the rivers.

雨水是梦中的疼痛
慢慢在呼吸中康复

Rain is the pain of dreams
slowly restored to health in breath.

雨声像梵音
一直到天明

Like monks chanting sutras
the rain goes on sounding right up to the break of day.

2010—2014

Art

Restriction and Creation — Thoughts upon Reading Meibing's Recent Oil Paintings

Cao Yiqiang / 曹意强
Translated by Maya Kovskaya

Cao Yiqiang / 曹意强

From a theoretical perspective, freedom and openness are the necessary conditions for artistic creation. It affords artists more choice and greater autonomy. In practice, however, this beneficial condition also increases the difficulty of making choices and judgments for artists. In the relatively closed environment of the art world, artists must work within specific stylistic restrictions. Their systems of reference and criteria for judgment are relatively clear-cut. This is similar to competitive sports, wherein athletes must exhibit their individual skills within the context of strict rules and make their breakthroughs within the restrictions set by the game. Meibing and I are the same age. Our generation of artists lived through the most isolated period in the history of modern Chinese art. Later, with Reform and Opening, we entered the most exciting era and enjoyed an unprecedented degree of intellectual and creative freedom. These two extreme situations put different demands on art, forcing artists to make different choices in each kind of context.

In 1978, Meibing was accepted into the Oil Painting Department of Nanjing Art Institute. After graduation in 1982, he began teaching at Nanjing Normal University. During the years of his studies, Chinese oil painting, as a discipline, was dominated by the realistic style of the "former Soviet Union." The works of Ilya Repin and Vasily Surikov were our models for learning, and *Spark Pictorial* was the only foreign art material that we could get our hands on and hungrily devoured. The predecessors of our admiration, such as Jin Shangyi (靳尚谊) and Zhan Jianjun (詹建俊), were contemporary Chinese oil painters who carried on the legacy of the Soviet School. Our *Jiangnan* painters learned from the artists who had returned to China, such as Quan Shanshi (全山石) and Xu Minghua (徐明华), the essence of the Soviet painting: emphasis on sketch shading , stress on drawing from life and sketching, and attention to tonal harmony in color. As a

Sweet Flag Oil on canvas 2017

student, Meibing's drawings, oil paintings, and sketches were all designed in pursuit of these effects.

An important fountainhead of the so-called Soviet painting was French Impressionism. At the end of the 1970s, a 19th-century French countryside landscape exhibition was held in Shanghai. It gave young people thirsting for Western oil paintings a chance to appreciate the original works of Manet, Pissarro, and Sisley with their own eyes. It was a visual feast beyond their imaginings! It had a huge impact on each of us, and our style of painting. Meibing was no exception. In his oil paintings, he became more attentive to the change and transparency of color, and his sketches became more free-flowing, showing the effect of this historical exhibition on his work.

During that period, because of limited exposure, a tendency toward a unified style was inevitable. Although this state of things played a role in curbing individuality, to a certain extent, it also established a strict criterion for judging the quality of art of a given category. Within the measures of the same category, as the saying goes, distinguishing the good from the bad should be self-evident.

Morning Mist Oil on canvas 2014

Now we have entered an era in which individuality is worshipped. Many people mistakenly take individuality to be an important factor in motivating artistic innovation. In fact, regardless of how much one imitates, the traces of one's individuality cannot be erased. It was in the course of a life of emulating Velasques that Manet finally became Manet. Who could have imagined that the modern masters, famed for their individual styles, such as the abstract expressionist Jackson Pollock, once tirelessly copied El Greco, or that Lucian Freud's favorite was Marc Chagall! Clearly imitation did not stifle the artistic personality of the imitators. Individuality is a neutral factor, and style is a category of art. Individuality and style can be distinguished in terms of good and bad, high and low, but cannot be conflated with art itself, much less be used as a value standard for judging artistic quality. By nature everyone possesses individuality, and each naturally has one's own style. Individual personality is like a wild horse. Indulging in individuality does not make one an artist. The real artist disciplines the individuality of that wild horse. The aforementioned great masters who emulated other great

An Aged Socialite of Bygone Days Oil on canvas 2016

masters learned to suppress their own nature in order to achieve a more ideal style and quality of painting. It is not a mark of one's artistic genuineness to stick to one's own individual style. Some Chinese painters misunderstood the slogan chanted by the romanticists that art demands artists be faithful to their own, blindly showing off their individuality, and pursuing distinctive styles. On the contrary, in this way they in fact lost themselves and lost the genuineness of their art. Instead, genuineness in art requires the steadfast courage to constantly exceed and overcome oneself, the object of one's expression, and the limitations of the media. Every artist must be honest with the content he expresses, namely, nature, and the inspiration or emotion inspired by it, and the skills that enable one to express that nature and those emotions. This is the way since time immemorial. The classical work of literary criticism: *Wen Xin Diao Long* (《文心雕龙》or *The Literary Mind and the Carving of Dragons*) posits "feeling," "matter," "language," as the "three standards." "Feeling" is inspiration, "matter" is the object, and "language" inheres in the performance skills and media available for use. Feelings are moved by matter, and language inspires feelings. "Language must take care of the heart, and the heart must be subsidiary to the matters, and the three accord with one another without overstepping the boundary in between." This is also applicable to painting, and the right path for artistic creators to follow.

However, in the art world of today, there are many works which fail to attend more care to this, thus lacking a balance amongst these three factors. There are painters who disproportionately seek novel techniques without having content of substance, who depict objects without affection, vent their emotions, and make drawings without meaning.

One obvious problem with contemporary Chinese oil painting is that most of the works lack things that can move a person. This demonstrates that the artist himself has lost his own

Objets E'art of Huizhou   Oil on canvas   2017

sensitivity to things. Meibing, however, always adheres to the principle of the "three standards." He does not forget to draw inspiration from nature and sharpen his sensitivity to things. His 2008 painting on the occasion of the heavy snowfall seen through his window is a good example. The transfer of that inspiration and sensitivity to the canvas must be based on skillful technique. Meibing's study of the history of color within the context of Western oil painting history was substantial.

He learned from the techniques of Titian, Rembrandt, Cézanne, and Modigliani. In 1996, he traveled to the United States and had the opportunity to study closely Western masterpieces at various museums. At the time, he was making landscape paintings that were deeply loved by Westerners and after his solo exhibition the lot was sold out. He combined 18th-century Italian landscape painting techniques with the colors of French Impressionism and Cézanne's space and structure, together with his unique sensitivity to exotic countries, giving his paintings a special atmosphere. Maybe Meibing himself did not realize one of the reasons why people favored his works was that the tableaux he created at that time employed a composition that appeared sloping and slightly unstable, and a deep and transparent coldness, all of which implied a certain indescribable mystery, a kind of feeling that one finds in the works of Goya, and even the grimness and secretiveness of a El Greco painting. This strange and subtle atmosphere also permeates Meibing's photographs. The demeanor of the characters and the life of the scene are instantaneously frozen in the magical light and shade that he effects. Only a keen eye can capture this sensitive moment of life. These photographic works, like his paintings, have become artworks with independent aesthetic values.

Meibing acknowledged the limitations of nature, one's own individual personality, as well as traditional media, and yet insisted on creating oil paintings on canvas. For him, the artist's creativity lies not in the act of innovating, but rather is embodied in the ability to fuse new things with seemingly incompatible things. Since China's Reform and Opening, more and more possibilities have been unfolding before Chinese artists, causing many people to lose their way in the swamp of too many choices. From the perspective of Xu Beihong (徐悲鸿) to today's Chinese artists, the ideal they obsess with is to create Chinese-style oil painting. This ideal inspires people to

The Guide Map Oil on canvas 2016

explore the possibility of an integration between Chinese and Western styles. At the same time, it can also lead to a tendency to ignore the intrinsic characteristics particular to oil painting in order to pursue a superficial Chinese ethnic style. In the open world of modern art, artists inevitably face the dilemma of what post-modern theorists call "double decoding." This "double decoding" has horizontal and vertical bi-directionality. Looking laterally, any artist must deal with the relationship between his national culture and the globalized art, that is, he or she must work in the field of vision of world art. Looking longitudinally, he or she must deal with the relationship between creation and tradition, that is, the artist must be engaged in contemporary creation within the traditional framework in which he is located. This horizontal and vertical "double decoding" is intertwined. It can be said that the success or failure of modern painters lies just in their efforts to "decode" . The modern art treats innovation as an absolute necessity. After a burst of creativity, this way reveals its weaknesses. When innovation comes to an end, it is difficult to imagine a newer style. The only way out is to return to tradition. Postmodernism is the result. However, post-modernism often misappropriates traditions with a cynical gesture, without ever intending to draw wisdom by studying the essence of tradition. In fact, any painter who works within a traditional framework will inevitably be influenced by the atmosphere of the times in which he lives.

Meibing's recent paintings have a unique postmodernist flavor. He expressed a traditional Chinese classical spirit through his smooth oil painting techniques. A pair of middle-aged man and woman sits beside a crude stone table admiring pine and plum bonsai there. There is a high, deep wall that reminds one of antiquity in its style and taste. In this environment, a dialogue between recent history and a more distant past is taking place, reflecting the border where the two meet, as embodied in the Emperor Zhao Ji's masterpiece *Ting Qin Tu*.(《听琴图》 or *Listening to the Chinese Zither*) This is also the dialogue between Chinese classical poetry and modern oil painting language. Meibing grew up in a scholarly family steeped in the study of Chinese classical literature. He had particular feelings about Chinese ancient culture and art, China's cultural relics — Qin and Han lacquer wares, carvings of the Tang and Song Dynasties, furniture of the Ming and Qing Dynasties, etc. — and he was familiar with these treasures and had exceptional insights about them. He also liked to enjoy *Jiangnan* lake stones, as well as bonsai, and loved amusing himself with literati's four treasures of the study (brush, ink stick, slab and paper). These kinds of hobbies and interests not only found full expression in his recent works, but also elevated the level of his art. Nowadays, a refined and learned man like Meibing is quite rare. His paintings are like his true self — when I first saw his works, I had such an impression. The painting *Magnolia* (《玉兰花》) that I saw then possessed elegant hues and the poetic white flowers, create a wonderful

The State of Mind Oil on canvas 2007

image that was intangible, both a flower and yet not a flower.

In this, another important teacher-student relationship for Meibing was revealed. One of his mentors was Su Tianci (苏天赐), an outstanding standard bearer among contemporary Chinese oil painters. If we say that the integration of Chinese and Western features to create distinctive Chinese-style oil paintings is the common ideal of several generations of their predecessors, then Su Tianci is one of the few painters who have come close to achieving this ideal. His works are redolent with the sensibilities of Chinese poetry, without losing touch with the characteristics of the medium of oil painting. Meibing's oil paintings also considerably brushwork of his teacher. Su Tianci painted flowers and captured the charming appeal of flowers through his distinctive brushstrokes. In his paintings, flowers are brushstrokes, brushstrokes are flowers, colors are flowers, flowers are colors — media, objects and images are fused in the furnace of his creativity. Meibing inherited the essence handed down from his master teacher, and more than that, he integrated the elements of impressionism and expressionism in the harmonious color scheme of Teacher Su. Meibing's *Lilies* (《百合花》) painted this year, is like the dance of a white fairy in the wind. The rectangular celadon

The Spring in Zhaji Oil on canvas 2017

vase and the thick green leaf cluster play a role in stabilizing the flying flowers, making them appear as stillness within movement, and emphasizing the charm of Chinese painting as well as the vivid tactile feel of oil painting.

In private exchanges with Meibing, we often explore the problem of why Chinese oil paintings so often lack the feeling of an "oil painting." From the perspective of the history of European oil painting, great oil painters use form and structure, or physique, to portray a sense of life, tactile qualities, and the musicality of color; they fully utilize the beauty of oil painting materials to create lifelike, breathing, touchable, and acoustic forms and bodies. Kandinsky said: "Real oil paintings often make people want to 'touch' them, because they have such life and tactility." And Renoir said that when he was painting, he would carefully consider where to put each color so as to allow it to perform its high tone. Meibing's recent works have made gratifying efforts in these areas, placing even more stress than before on exploring the charm of oil painting language. *Shuang Song Dui Yu* (《双松对语》or *Dialogue between Two Pine Trees*) is an excellent case in point. In the picture, each of the objects depicted — the pine branches, pine leaves, ancient stone tables, rockery stones, courtyard gates, courtyard walls, and spotlight figures — are full of the brushstrokes and colors of life rhythms and sound sensations. Here, as in the *Lilies* auditory and visual sensations are all played out in the work.

Synesthesia — to see through sounds or to experience sounds as shapes — is not unique to Western aesthetics. Ancient Chinese people also stress the experience of synesthesia from tactile and auditory senses. In *The Correct Interpretation of Classics* (《礼记正义》), a section of Kong Yingda's (孔颖达) commentary on "The Book of Music" (《礼记·乐记》) states: "The sound can move people, since it makes people imagine its shape." In his *Flute Rhapsodies* (《长笛赋》) Ma Rong (马融), of the Eastern Han Dynasties, once wrote even more clearly: "You can associate the sound with a certain shape — it is like flowing water, and resembles a flying wild swan." I don't know if Meibing has consciously sought to relate to these traditional aesthetic experiences in his oil painting creations, but looking at his recent works naturally reminds me of this.

The uniqueness of Meibing's art lies in his exploration of the expressiveness of oil paintings with classic Chinese themes. While expressing his musings over the past, he fuses different carriers and media into an excuse for experimental painting. For example, in *Frolicking Children* (《婴戏图》), the painter borrows the dynamic composition from its Song Dynasty genre painting, and displays plausible rhythms, light perceptions, and fluid movement that reveal the "forcign flavor" of oil painting.

Meibing created an incredibly large number of works in the second half of this year. The various tableaux can be summed up in a single theme: "Dialogue." At night under the moon, the tea lover sits alone at the lakeside talking with nature. Under the moonlit tree, the Buddhist Arhat dialogues with a monkey, and the smoker sits leisurely in front of a folding screen and converses with "literati's four treasures of the study." The monk sits in lotus position in the curling smoke of incense and dialogues with his faith. There are depictions other more obvious forms of dialogues as well. This dialogue is actually a tête-à-tête between the painter himself and the two different traditions — China and the West — on two temporal dimensions — the present and the past. In accordance with the popular post-modern discourse, this is the most modernistic pattern of dual dialogues: on the one hand, it is a modern interpretation of Chinese classical spirit, and on the other hand, by deciphering the essence, it firmly grasps the essential characteristics of the artistic language of foreign oil painting. In this heterogeneous dialogue, the past and present, the Chinese spirit and the Western discourse have transcended one another to achieve harmony. Meibing's classical tastes enable this transformation of the past into modernity, that is, he makes it possible from the perspective of modern people to savor and associate the characteristics of an ancient Chinese sentiment. He uses oil painting as a vehicle for expressing this, and thus approaches a state that Baudelaire described: *The past is fascinating, not only because the artist can abstract from it a beauty that belongs to the present, but precisely because it belongs to the past; it has historical value. The present is also like that. We get pleasure from the present. This is not merely because the moment can be endowed with beauty, but also because it becomes the intrinsic characteristic of the moment.*

Only those people who think about the remote history and embrace the wide world can appreciate this beauty: the beauty of oil painting created by sincere respect for the restrictions imposed by tradition, modernity, and the art media itself. Restrictions are not a limitation on creation, but a necessary condition for creation. The poet T.S. Eliot once said that there are only three truly talented poets in the world: Dante, Shakespeare, and Goethe. He described them as creative as God, and said that their creations embody the universal and lofty humanity that is understood by all human beings. When Dante completed the final song of the great *Divine Comedy*, he made the following prayers to God:

> *O Light Supreme, that dost uplift Thyself*
> *so far from mortal thought, relend my mind*
> *a little of what Thou didst seem to be,*
> *and cause my tongue to be so powerful,*
> *that of Thy Glory it may leave at least*
> *a spark unto the people still to come ...*[1]

Genius Dante understands that creation from nothingness is also creation from the unrestricted, which is the exclusive power of God alone. Mortal creativity is nothing but a humble addition to God's creation. Human creativity must use existing, available resources and change their form and effect in unexpected ways. Creativity requires imagination, not simple innovation and unlimited freedom. Creativity itself is a limitation. Anything creative and original must satisfy two seemingly contradictory conditions at the same time. On the one hand, it is necessary to break norms in unpredictable and novel ways. On the other hand, it must be widely accepted and appreciated sooner or later and becomes a new norm. In other words, innovation must go against the normal way of thinking, and yet it must ultimately be understood by normal thinking. The originality of pure individuality is quirky eccentricity rather than genuine creativity. Meibing, like other modern Chinese painters, enjoys unprecedented creative freedom, and freedom and restriction are both prerequisites to artistic creation. From our conversations, I got the feeling that Meibing realized that freedom in art is neither arrogance nor laissez-faire. It can only be achieved by transcending the restrictions imposed by art itself, that is, wisely bringing the achievements of previous generations, artistic media, and individual temperament into consideration in order to mold something new and thus attaining freedom. The development of Western oil painting has always been rooted in portraiture. When speaking of oil painting, human figure is not only the subject matter but also the form itself that matters. Therefore, whether the human figures are painted well or not should be the basic standard by which one judges the quality of a painting. In other words, in the history of oil painting, due to the absolute position occupied by the human figure, the techniques of oil painting were primarily invented and developed around the task of painting the human figure. If you do not have the chops to paint a human figure, then you have not really mastered the techniques of oil painting. Jean-Baptiste-Siméon Chardin is a still life giant, Jean-Baptise-Camille Corot and Camille Pissarro are landscape masters, but they all prove their extraordinary talents of composition and expression through their outstanding rendering of the human figure. In order to further improve himself, Meibing has recently begun to study the techniques of portraiture and figure sketching. The works he has painted in recent times have absorbed the techniques of famous artists such as Renoir and paid attention to the interaction of form, color, and brushstrokes. In this way, the picture becomes more full and brimming. Here, Meibing uses tradition to impose higher requirements on himself to standardize his own art. We know that every true artist in the world will pursue freedom with the same awareness of the restrictions imposed by art in order to transcend them. We look forward to Meibing's continuing efforts. Each step solidly approaches this realm of ideal creation.

››› Translator's Notes:

1. Dante, Alighieri, *The Divine Comedy, Vol.2 (Paradiso)* English Trans. Courtney Langdom: Harvard University Press [1321/1921]: 391.